NOTHING BUT PRAIRIE AND SKY

NOTHING BUT

Recorded by WALKER D. WYMAN
from the original notes of BRUCE SIBERTS

Norman:

PRAIRIE AND SKY

LIFE ON THE DAKOTA RANGE
IN THE EARLY DAYS

UNIVERSITY OF OKLAHOMA PRESS

BY WALKER D. WYMAN:

Nothing But Prairie and Sky (Norman, 1954)
California Emigrant Letters (New York, 1952)
The Wild Horse of the West (Caldwell, Idaho, 1945)
*A Topical Guide to the Mississippi Valley Historical Review
and Proceedings* (Mississippi Valley Historical
Association, 1934)

Library of Congress Catalog Card Number: 54-5930

NOTHING BUT PRAIRIE AND SKY

BACK IN the fall of 1945 I received a letter from Mr. Bruce Siberts, of Okmulgee, Oklahoma, a person then unknown to me, saying that he had read my book *The Wild Horse of the West,* that he had done considerable mustanging himself when he was a rancher in South Dakota, and that he believed his experiences might be of interest to people today.

In the correspondence that followed, Mr. Siberts asked me to help him tell the story of his life west of the Missouri. Though I was somewhat in doubt about this project, I encouraged him to write a few pages about his early experiences as a horse and cattle rancher. This he did at once and when I had read it, I was convinced that his life's story was worth putting together if we could ever get it on paper. I suggested certain procedures and organization and asked him to start writing or dictating, and to send me a few pages at a time. These pages were recorded verbatim, then I would write him to comment on what I thought was interesting, ask for more information on some point, or suggest that he not concern himself with this or that type of experience. As he wrote, the story improved. When he finished in October, 1950, he had produced over 900 pages in longhand—all of it written while Siberts was between the ages of seventy-seven and eighty-two.

In the spring of 1950, I went to Oklahoma to spend some time with Mr. Siberts. We went over the typescript, clearing up a point here, expanding an idea there. As important as the amplification was the opportunity to learn his language habits and especially to hear his salty speech in action.

This is Bruce Siberts' story, not as he wrote it but as he might have written it had his experiences been in the world of writing rather than ranching. While he was a literate man who read extensively, his writings were short on those matters discussed in freshman composition. Consequently, there is hardly a sentence in this book that is exactly as he wrote it. Paragraphs have been pieced together out of scattered items, and chapters have been created by a liberal rearrangement of the story. I have put words in his mouth hundreds of times but have never invented an incident. Much that he wrote about his life has been omitted. In fact, all that I have done in rewriting and rearranging has been to give it a sense of unity, a more orderly development, and upon occasion, I hope, a more readable way of saying something.

Here, then, is one man's adventures on the upper Plains as rewritten by one far removed in the sense of chronology and geography. In one sense, it is a history of the open range after the drawing of the last frontier line in 1880. In many respects, it is good social history of that last frontier process. Perhaps much of it is folklore and, upon occasion, it is probably just tall-tale. Even if it is one or all of these, a reader can come away from the book with a greater appreciation of what life was like when there was "nothing but prairie and sky" west of the Missouri.

Bruce Siberts had a keen sense of history and a recognition that the nation had long since passed the point of no return as far as its pioneer period was concerned. His awareness of the part played by little men in the conquest of the continent created in him a hunger to see his own record in sober print. Unfortunate it is that fate has denied this to him, for in October, 1952, this pioneer passed on to a new frontier where, it is said, there are no rustlers, blizzards, or alkali water. *Nothing But Prairie and Sky*, therefore, stands as a memorial to one who once rode the range and in so doing wrote his own preface to the Republic of our time.

WALKER D. WYMAN

Wisconsin State College
River Falls, Wisconsin
February 22, 1954

NOTHING BUT PRAIRIE AND SKY

TABLE OF CONTENTS

xi

NOTHING BUT PRAIRIE AND SKY

ILLUSTRATIONS

xiii

NOTHING BUT PRAIRIE AND SKY

THE COOK was a windjammer if I ever heard one. He kept spinning his yarns as we squatted on our haunches around the campfire that cold night in the fall roundup of 1901. He said he had been in Africa, Australia, and China as a sailor and in South America as a ranch hand, and from his stories I believe he might have been.

He spit into the fire, rolled another cigaret, and told about the 400-pound streetwalker called Harriet Lane who was so popular on the water front in Sydney. Well, when she died, the undertaker was in trouble as the corpse was too big for any coffin he had. A friend of the undertaker's who owned a meat-packing plant offered to help him out. He had plenty of 200-pound kegs used for packing bully beef in brine, so they trimmed old Harriet down, packed her in a couple of them, and stenciled her name on the heads. Somehow, these barrels got mixed up with the others and went to sea as bully beef. When the boat came back to port, old Harriet Lane was no longer aboard.

This cook's story is not all that I remember about the eighty-two years I have lived. I first saw the light of day on

November 21, 1868, in Winfield, Iowa. At the age of twen-ty-two, I beat it out to the Black Hills to make my fortune, worked around for a year or two, and finally became a cattle and horse rancher myself. I have done a lot of bad things in my life, but I never did stoop to sheep ranching. The range country west of the Missouri didn't have much in it but prairie and sky and livestock in the sixteen years I was there, but I got along pretty well. I drank enough alkali water to rust my pipes, made some money raising horses, got into a number of scrapes, and all in all, got pretty well acquainted with what pioneer life was like on the last American fron-tier.

As a child in Iowa, I was sickly, had croup, measles, or something all the time, so they tell me, and there was doubt if I would ever make it. I was sometimes called the snot-nosed brat, which was probably a pretty good description. I did not like to be washed, but on Sunday before we went to church the folks would catch me and give me a going over. Pa would take a pan of water, a wash cloth, and a handful of old homemade soft soap and start in. How I hated that soap. He would hold me with one hand, slap the runny soap on my head, and start rubbing. My two sisters would laugh and holler. Ma would tell Pa to wash the ears and neck, which he would do for ten minutes, and then the both of them would stand me in a tub of water. Pa was thorough and seemed to enjoy the show, but I would bawl and howl all the time until they finally decided I was clean and fit for public appearance.

We would then get dressed and be on our way to Sun-day school. Pa was superintendent and Ma played the or-gan. I liked Sunday school. A half-witted boy who winked and made faces at one old man helped make it interesting. Old man McCallister also made this a worth-while expe-rience. He would march in with a stovepipe hat on, sit down

4

and take off his hat, pull out a big red handkerchief, and blow a blast on it that made the rafters ring.

Religion was a pretty serious matter to me. I did not want to go to Hell, which the preacher described as a place of torment and a burning, fiery furnace. I wanted to keep out if possible. In Sunday school I learned "Now I Lay Me Down to Sleep," The Lord's Prayer, and the Ten Commandments. I understood all of the Ten Commandments but one—Thou shall not commit adultery. Once when the preacher was eating dinner at our house I asked him what it meant. He was slow about answering so I told him I thought it was adulterating food like tea and coffee, and my parents hurriedly agreed with this meaning. I told a good many lies but mostly got caught at it. We had lots to eat but I would steal cookies and other sweet stuff. Pa used to say that I was full of the Devil and that "by the Old Harry, I will tan your hide." This was a bluff I found out. I think he had high hopes for me, but I knew I was a bad boy and would do any kind of devilment I thought safe.

Our family were strict Methodists, attended church regular, and none of them ever got drunk, chewed or smoked tobacco, or used bad language. Only Uncle Ed, who bought cattle and hogs for the Chicago market, was different. He chewed tobacco, was suspected of drinking beer once, and had the reputation of seeing a show in Chicago called "The Black Crook," in which women wore tights. As Uncle Ed and Mr. Crum, a neighbor, were the only Methodists who used tobacco, except on the sly, it was urged that they be expelled from the church. But in looking over the records, it was learned that they were the best in paying money for the support of the church and so they were allowed to remain in good standing. However, the minister preached a strong sermon on the evils of tobacco, saying, "There you sit with hell juice running out of your mouths," and on in

5

that line for two hours. Uncle Ed said that the preacher could kiss his foot and go to hell. Only he didn't say foot.

Grandpa Henry Siberts, who had come to Iowa from Maryland after having been a cordwainer's apprentice there, was strong in faith. He was frequently called upon to pray, always repeating the same prayer he delivered at meals and before going to bed, only a lot louder. In the summertime when the doors and windows of the church were open, you could hear him all over town. He also took his politics very seriously. One time after an election he said that both Texas and Hell had gone Democratic. This was the only bad word I ever heard him say.

My Pa was born in Beaver County, Pennsylvania, in 1839, and was given the handle of Cyrus. He was a veteran of the Civil War, having fought with the Fifth Iowa Volunteers and Forty-fifth Iowa Infantry and marched with Sherman to the sea. He still had his blue army overcoat with yellow-lined cape in 1877. When I was about five, another ex-soldier came to see him. They were in the barn talking about their march across Georgia. Sam, the visitor, had been a captain and recalled his adventures with a yellow gal in Savannah. There was a lot of detail that I did not understand. Pa said to Sam, "Little pitchers have big ears," but both were so interested in the subject that they forgot to pay any attention to me. I wanted a little more information about the matter, so after Sam had left and we were eating supper, I asked Pa and Ma what a yellow gal was. Ma got up and went to the kitchen, slammed the door, came back, and slammed it again. She told Pa he should be ashamed of himself for such talk and told me that the soldiers were in the war to free all the slaves, including the yellow ones. Pa made the best alibi he could, but Ma was cross at him for several days. He told me I had better learn to keep my mouth shut. This advice I have never been able to follow.

6

Pa was quite sudden sometimes. One morning when it was cold and snowing, he told me to bring in the wood while he went out to milk and to feed the stock. When he came in and saw the woodbox still bare, he asked me why I had not got the wood. I told him I couldn't get my boots on. He grabbed me with one hand and my boots with the other and threw me and the boots out the door. The snow on the ground sure made the boots go on easy. They had to stop me when the woodbox was full and some was piled on the floor.

Ma was the daughter of Sherman Terry and Ann Bruce Terry, descendants of the Maryland Scotch-Irish. She was born in Kossuth, Iowa, where the first college in the state was located. Her family was strong on education and literary studies, her father being one of the founders of the college. Ma had one of the first organs in our town, studied rhetoric, grammar, music, painting, and Latin, and took *Godey's Ladies Book*. My family subscribed for the Chicago *Inter-Ocean* and *Youth's Companion*. Grandpa took the Toledo *Blade*. Pa enjoyed reading Shakespeare out loud. Ma liked all of it except the coarse words.

I started to school at five. The building was known as Smoky Hall since the walls and the ceilings had been badly smoked from a smoky stove. It stayed that way as long as I was in school. I got along well in school, learning how many bones there were in the human body—208 without the teeth —and the names of some of them. Most of the work was on the three R's, readin', 'ritin', and 'rithmetic. Spelling was also taught by having spelling bees. If sparing the rod spoils the child, none of us was ever spoiled in school.

When I was a lad in the 1870's, farming wasn't exactly a quick way to get rich. Prices of farm produce were low and farmers were dissatisfied, many of them joining the new semi-secret society, the Grange. Crops were poor since there was no tiling or draining of the low areas, and Caanan town-

7

ship had so much swamp that Pa said some of the people had webfeet. Many people gave up the ghost and headed for the West to start out again.

About this time Grandpa Terry got the asthma and went to Kansas where the air was drier. He left an old mare with us when he went. Old Fan was what you would call a family mare, was thirty years old, and so temperamental that she kicked the sides of the barn out just for exercise. After she had kicked out one side of her stall, Pa put two-inch oak boards in and told her to kick as long as she wanted to. Sometimes we would wake up in the night and hear her banging away with both back feet. Fifteen minutes was about all she could go at one time, maybe because her feet got bruised. Once Pa threatened to shoot Old Fan but Ma wouldn't let him, said we had promised Grandpa to keep her until she died. She was my pet saddle horse. I would get an old bridle on her and ride in the pasture until she got so tired she laid down. Pa scolded me for riding her so much but I told him she needed exercise. We kept her three or four years before we found her dead in the barn one morning. That was one night we didn't hear her kicking the daylights out of the stall. Ma cried at the loss of this old family friend, but I'll bet the old devil kicked the ridge pole out of her stall in the happy hunting ground.

Ma liked to have things stylish, so when I was five she bought me a pair of women's stockings with red, green, yellow, and blue stripes around. She also got some goods to make me a coat. One day she took me and the cloth into Winfield to a fancy dressmaker named Dade Hinckle. Having no pattern for a boy's coat except a basque, Mrs. Hinckle cut one from that. It would have fit a woman pretty well but on me it bulged out in front. In the back it flowed out to make room for a bustle. It was a fine piece of work, no doubt, but when we took it home and tried it on with the striped

8

stockings, I was a sight for sore eyes. Pa did not say anything when he first saw me, just stood there and shook his head. Ma made me wear this outfit even though the boys made fun of me. Even when the day was cold, I would tell Ma that I was hot and not wear it. Finally Pa got tired of looking at this show and shelled out $4.50 for my first suit of store clothes. I was quite proud of this and put on a lot of style around my friends who had made fun of my bustle coat.

HARDLY a country boy of my generation could see any future on an Iowa farm. It was fun, of course, to ride the calves and roam the countryside, to eat big meals at threshing time, and to be treated like a man by Ma and Pa long before I was. But the excitement of watching a yearling grow up day by day could not compete with the excitement of digging for gold in the Rockies or trailing a herd from Texas to Montana. The Black Hills was a center of wild tales during all my boyhood, and when I was ten, three of us youngbloods started to go there but gave it up after walking fifteen or twenty miles one hot day. By the time I was twenty-two, I decided that the West was the place for me, and headed for the land of adventure.

It was on the evening of July 8, 1890, that I climbed on a baggage car at Mount Pleasant, Iowa, and started out. On the same car was a boy going from New York to Frisco. At Ottumwa three bums, drunk as lords, got on and started acting mean. One of them chased us up on top, yelling throw them under the wheels. A low pass under a viaduct caught one of them and off he went screaming bloody murder as he fell. We never found out what happened to him. The other bums got off at the next stop, but we went on as we were afraid we might be blamed for a murder.

In Omaha I heard about the good wages being paid by the Burlington, then building a line between Deadwood and

Siding Seven, so I went to a dingy office where I paid the agent two dollars and was given a ticket out to my new job. The next day I climbed into a special car loaded with as fine a collection of hoboes, greenhorns, and drunks as I had ever seen. The next day we arrived at Siding Seven, a settlement of tents and shanties, later known as Edgemont, South Dakota. This was a pretty bad place. Drunks were everywhere. Joy girls paraded with little on except paint. Pimps were busy lining up business. A man running an eating-house hollered at me, asking me if I wanted a job washing dishes. I asked one of my new pals, big Jim, what I should do. He said he would see about it, went in, and took the job himself. That night I slept on the warehouse platform along with about two hundred Chinese, Cornish men, Negroes, and general bums who had either come in on my car or had quit their jobs and were hoping to snatch a free ride out. To get out of the Black Hills that summer one had to walk or pay fare, as every train had special bouncers to throw a man off.

After breakfast, a railroad man came along and picked twelve of us for a job. As we lumbered along the surveyed roadbed, a tinhorn gambler told how he skinned the green ones in poker, and the hardrock men told their stories. That night in camp we had a supper that was a sight—bread, meat, and potatoes—and all that we could eat. We slept in a long bunkhouse on loose hay. Each man was given a blanket but no pillow. There were more than just men in that bunkhouse, and I was scratching most of the night. All the old hands were lousy as pet coons but didn't seem to mind this extra baggage. An interesting and elevating pastime was to take a louse from one man and pitch him in battle against one from another man. Being strangers they fought until one killed the other. As one old bum said, the bunkhouse was no place for a minister's son or daughter to grow up.

The next morning after a good breakfast, eight of the

twelve who had come the day before took one last look around and high-tailed it out of the country on shanks' mares. The boss was fit to be tied, and he cussed them as long as they were in sight. The rest of us—two old hardrock men and the two pilgrims, the gambler, and myself—were taken out to the place where the Lord had put too many mountains, and we were to help move them. Three hardrock men worked together, one holding a drill between his knees while the other two swung their sledges. It looked risky to me, but we had no mis-licks as long as I was there. We two greenhorns were issued a pick, shovel, and wheelbarrow, and told to get to work moving the dirt and rock that had been blasted out. My wheelbarrow was a rickety concern and would tip over and spill my load. The boss thought it was my fault and fired me the next day. I was glad he did, for I had no hankering to be one of the many floaters who were buried under the debris that summer.

I started up the trail to the north as soon as I could get going. At Custer there was a lot of excitement over the finding of a nugget worth $150. One old miner there whose claim was not paying well let me stay all night in his wagon. He had been all around, in Africa, Australia, Mexico, and California, and had property in the East. His cabin was clean and full of books and papers. Nor was he lousy. He told me how to get rid of them by putting my clothes on an anthill first, then boiling them. In the winter, clothing could be soaked and hung out to freeze. These pests were common in most camps, and bedbugs were in practically all hotels and houses I was ever in west of the Missouri River. Some people burnt sulphur to fumigate a room, even if the fumes bleached the clothing. Most people just scratched.

The next day I got to Hill City, a little Black Hills settlement that like all the others called itself a city and hoped to be the center of the universe within a few years. Everybody was talking about how a grizzly bear had killed a man near the Etta Mine. A lot of men were either coming into town to spend their money or were going from one job to another farther on. Many of them had no place to stay so built fires and lay on the ground. I got a place at a boarding camp one night and the next stayed in the barn at a small mine. The boss and his wife were nice people. They had five men working for them, had found some good ore and some tin, but they were nearly out of money. The woman had a little organ, and she played and sang for us that night. When I started on north the next morning, she told me I would be better off if I went back to Iowa. At Deadwood City, where meals were about a dollar, I bought a can of cherries and a loaf of bread for my dinner, and as I ate it, I wondered if the woman wasn't right.

There was a lot of business at Deadwood and Lead. Since there was no railroad connection with the outside world, freighting was good business. The Northwestern Transportation Company had a lot of big wagons pulled by a string of horses or mules. A narrow-gauge railroad connected the two settlements and hauled the ore to the stamp mills. The Homestake Mine was the large one, and there was still quite a lot of placer mining done. Farmers, dairymen, and gardeners were doing pretty good. The livery business took a lot of grain and hay, and the miners stowed away a lot of food. At the outside of Deadwood were a lot of eight-by-ten shanties. I wandered down there the first night and from each doorway a Chinese woman would call to me to come in. A bunch of rowdy Cornish miners came by, and they advised me to stay away from the women. One old drunk said they had leperosity and other diseases. I got out pretty fast. I never did like a strong Chinese smell anyway.

After riding to Whitewood with a freighter and never being out of sight of wagons, stages, or men on foot, I went to a small hotel. The lady wanted me to stay up with a sick boy, offering me a two-dollar supper and breakfast. I took the job but was so tired and sleepy that I finally laid down across the bed and went to sleep. The boy woke me and wanted water, so I took the pitcher and went to a well in the street and got him some. He told me to go back to sleep and if he wanted anything he would kick and holler. The next morning he told me I was better than some who had waited on him as I was easier to wake up.

Falling in with three other young fellows that morning, I decided to go to Sturgis, then called Scooptown. It was a bad place filled at that time with soldiers from Fort Meade. Getting thirsty, we stopped at a farm to get some water. The woman said, "No water," but the man gave us a dipper and pulled a bucket full of water out of the dug well. Later one of the boys said we should wait until dark and go back and burn the woman's house down. But we thought that wouldn't be fair to the man. After sleeping in an oat shock that evening, we got into Rapid City the next day.

I was still looking for a job, but the prospects weren't so good in Rapid City where there were ten men for every job. I decided to go to Hot Springs so I bought a ticket to Buffalo Gap and walked from there. There I got located at a boarding and rooming house for $4.50 a week and found a job the next day mixing mortar for a plasterer at $2.25 a day. After being picked on by the carpenter's son for a few days, I quit and soon had work cleaning up around a new church college. I have always heard that you can't be both Christian and rich. Well, these people must have been Christians, for they fired us without paying any of our wages. I went every day for about a week trying to get my pay, but I never got any action until I threatened to turn the account over to a lawyer. Then they hustled the money. After that, I never had much to do with pokey and stubborn preacher outfits.

13

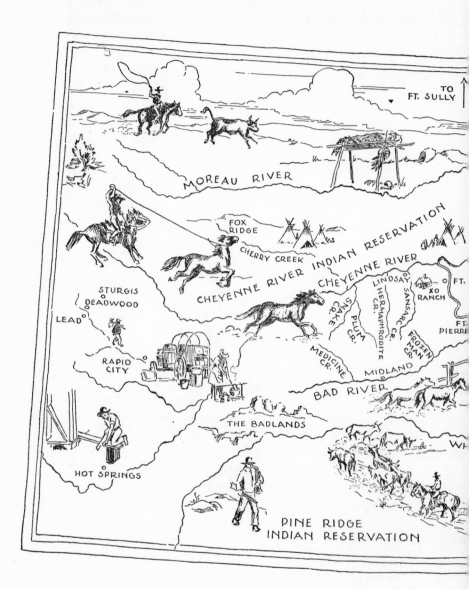

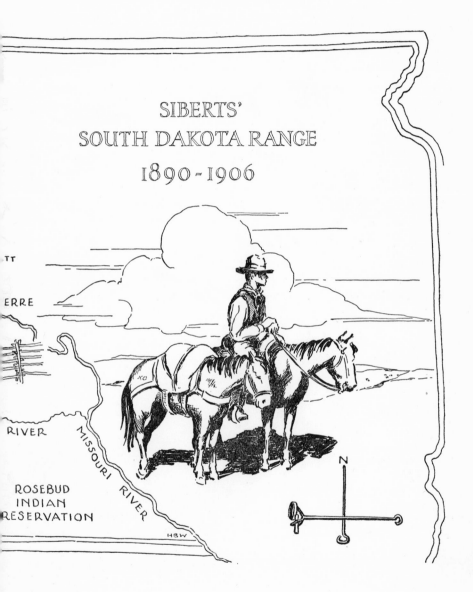

SIBERTS'
SOUTH DAKOTA RANGE
1890 ~ 1906

At Hot Springs I met Ben C. Ash, who had finished his part in the fight to win the support of the Black Hills people for moving the South Dakota capitol from Huron to Pierre. He had bought three hundred ranch horses and wanted me to help take them to Fort Pierre. I was tired of the Hills so took the job. We herded them during the day and penned them at night at road ranches along the way. We never saw a wire fence after leaving Rapid City, and very few horses and cattle made any use of that wonderful grassland we passed over. We crossed the Missouri about August 20, 1890, on a pontoon bridge, and in Ash's barn I had the best place to sleep I had had since I left Iowa. Maybe I had not found my fortune yet, but I had seen a lot of South Dakota's great pasture just waiting for a man to put some cattle in it. The railroad could hire, fire, and bury its bums, and the Welshmen could burrow into the Black Hills if they wanted to, but the Pierre country looked good to me and I decided to stay.

CHAPTER 2

THE PLUM CREEK INDIAN SCARE

PIERRE was a lively place in 1890. It had a population of six or seven thousand, and the speculators had laid out additions five or six miles from town. One speculator even advertised in the Sunday school papers. Both Pierre and Fort Pierre across the river were trading points for the Sioux, and a lot of them were coming and going all the time. Many of them were trying to get hold of the forty-four Winchester repeating rifles, model 1873. This was still the popular Winchester. There was some talk of an outbreak of the Sioux, who were surly and hateful, and some were doing the

Ghost Dance. Some of the white people remembered the Sioux trouble following the Custer Massacre and told stories of the killing and torture at that time. One old man told about a case he had seen. The white man had been staked down, his eyelids, nose, and penis cut off, and the latter stuck into his mouth. Of course, not all the whites were angels, but it wasn't exactly a comfortable feeling to know that the Sioux coming and going around Pierre would like to do that to the rest of us. Quite a few people went back east that fall, but I stayed and worked for Ash.

In an old frame building back of Ash's barn and corral was a Chinese laundry. One day when I was leading some broncs to water, a big kid on a bicycle rode up behind me and the horses stampeded and ran over me. It knocked me out, and I was a bloody, skinned-up mess. The Chinks got me in their house and doctored my scratches with some of their home remedies. After an hour or so, I bandaged my face with some of their clean cloths and went after my horses.

This Chinese family had a little girl about seven years old called Tocky. She was very cute. They dressed her like a white child and tried to send her to school, but the whites wouldn't have it. So she stayed close to their laundry. One day a couple of big kids chased her into the barn where I was and threatened to cut off her pigtail. I told the kids to skip out of there and that if I ever heard of them bothering Tocky again I would cut their ears off. They sneaked off like a dog with his tail between his legs. Tocky quit crying and yelled at them, "You a damned son of a bitch and you papa an old jackass." Her English showed that she had been to school a few days. The swear words she used, along with "bastard" as a close second, were useful to all of us in the western country, and I don't see what we would have done without them. I used to buy candy for Tocky, and I am sure she thought lots of me. Her parents were good people and

Bruce Siberts at the age of twenty-one

when they moved to Deadwood later made good in a store there. I don't know what ever became of Tocky.

When Ash was through with me that fall, he asked me what he owed me. I told him twenty dollars. He gave me fifty dollars, and with forty of it I bought an Indian pony and a saddle. Right after that I met Harvey and Charles Robinson. They were going to put in an Indian trading post at the Cheyenne City townsite at the mouth of Plum Creek about one hundred miles northwest of Pierre. The site was later known as Leslie Post Office. The Robinsons had a claim for a lot there, and I also got one at a cost of one dollar. Since it was across from the Cherry Creek subagency, it was a good place for the Indian trade, even though there were already two stores there. These Lakotas were friendly to traders and when they got their U. S. payments were good spenders.

The Robinsons had been educated as lawyers before coming out to this wild country to become horse ranchers. They had about two hundred ponies on the Oahe bottom northwest of Pierre. Henry Angel, who had a store at Cheyenne City, claimed the range about ten miles up and ten miles down the Cheyenne River and south to the Black Hills, about eight hundred square miles, for his herd of one hundred cattle. He was not friendly to us and tried to stop us from cutting hay on his range. The old pioneers were not modest in claiming things.

We got the Indians to cut and haul the cedar logs for building the store, paying about fifty cents a log. In about ten days we got a building up, twenty-by-twenty-feet square. While Charles and I went to Pierre to get goods, Harvey stayed there to hold possession. Harvey was the only one who was not a little scared of Angel. When we got back from Pierre eight days later with our goods, we found that the haystack had been burned. We then hired the Indian preacher, Edwin Phelps, who claimed a little draw about

19

three miles long, to cut some hay for our stock, and we spread some talk around that we would hang someone if this haystack burned. I also strengthened my life insurance by buying an ivory-handled Colt forty-five six-shooter. Having traded my old saddle for a first-class Menea made in Cheyenne, Wyoming, I began to think I was quite a fellow. In the 5,000-square-mile area, bounded on the south by the Black Hills–Pierre Trail, on the east by the Missouri, and on the north and west by the Cheyenne, were no more than forty whites. And one of them was trying to claim most of the country. Iowa was never like this.

I cut green logs and built a ten-by-ten cabin on my lot. For the roof I laid saplings against the ridge pole, then covered them with hay and about six inches of dirt. This was the usual house found in the whole Dakota country. Even the Indians built on this plan. They were warm in the winter and cool in the summer but bad when we had a rain.

Nearly every evening we could hear the Indians dancing and yelling in the White Thunder bottom up the river. They had built a big house about 60 by 100 feet at the camp where Hump's clan lived, and were talking war. They said they did not want to fight the traders but did want to kill the Okechata soldiers. I think it meant that some of the agents had not issued the amount of beef and flour that the treaties called for. When they would come into the store they would act all right, but when you met them outside they wouldn't speak to you but would cover up all their heads and faces except for one eye which they peeked out of. This made a person feel mighty queer when you knew there were about a thousand of them within thirty or forty miles.

The Robinsons had brought their wives, and Harvey had two boys about two and five years old. They sent them back to Pierre as soon as the trouble began to brew. We hauled all the goods in and sent all the horses, except one team and my pony, to the Oahe bottoms ranch. One of the traders pulled out, leaving only Angel, the Robinsons, and myself. It looked bad. The people in the towns were getting guns and sending out men to scout. Harvey thought we ought to get out, too, so we started south. At the old Plum Creek stage station on the Black Hills Trail we met a man on a white horse who was out scouting. He told us some scare stories about what they had seen when they were surveying the government lands about three miles away. At Lance Creek Holes we saw the surveying crew who told of a lot of shooting the night before at or near Plum Creek Station. They thought the Indians had attacked the place and killed the two men that were there, and were in a hurry to get out of the country. Each of them had a breech-loading musket and twenty brass cartridges which had been issued by the War Department to the settlers all over the country. I tried shooting mine for the first time just to see if it would work, but it kicked so hard that it hurt me worse than it would have hurt an Indian between the sights.

When we got to Pierre the next day, we learned that a bunch of white men had gone to the Plum Creek Station two days before and had shot off a lot of ammunition just to scare the surveyors. It had worked all right, as the government men had left behind a lot of tools, horse feed, a good tent, and other supplies and never went back for them. There hadn't been any Indians within miles of the place. People had a good laugh, and we quit worrying about being ambushed by the Sioux.

After spending two or three days at the Oahe bottom ranch where Henry, an older brother of the Robinson boys, had charge, we thought we had better go back to the store. Rev. Riggs of the Indian mission and church had a good-sized flatboat, and he and his hired men and all of us worked at the job of getting us across the Missouri. We took the wagon apart for loading and held a horse on each side of it. Four men took to the oars and we were off. By dark we were on the other side of the river, and by ten o'clock we were at Fred Fruh's place. Fred's Indian wife got supper for us. He had lived here since about 1866 and had cut wood for the steamboats as long as they ran up the river. Fred was a domino player, or muggins as he called it, and so we played with him until after twelve. For a pet he had a de-scented skunk which he fed as we ate our meal. He also had a flock of goats that would walk up the wagon tongue, climb into the wagon, and eat everything that happened to be in the wagonbox. I slept in the wagon that night to keep these rancid-smelling critters from getting in. They blatted all night and even made a good beginning on eating the canvas off the wagon. We had enough of his dominoes and goats and moved on the next day, but I often stopped at his place in later years. He liked to go into Pierre and get pretty full. Maybe that is why the old coot lived to be ninety-six before they put him under the sod.

We headed up the Standing Butte Road, guided by the old landmark, a 300-foot butte used so long by the Indians. There was a hole in the top where a watcher could hide and see a lot of country. We couldn't see any stock or anything for miles and miles around. That night we got to the junction of Sansarc Creek and the Cheyenne where Old Rattling Rib's camp used to be and the next day on to Fred Dupree's ranch. Fred was a French Canadian who had come to Dakota in 1838 with the Northwest Fur Company. Now he had an Indian wife and ten grown children. He ran about 2,000 horses and 4,000 cattle under the Circle D brand. Pete, his son, had fifteen or twenty buffalo at that time which he afterward sold to Scotty Phillip. This family lived in a twenty-by-forty-foot house and did pretty well. There were about forty in the family and usually a dozen drifters or

22

people passing through at mealtime. Old Eagle Brand canned milk was the biggest product from the outside world. The men ate first and the women and children later. None of them could speak English except old Fred, and he mixed it up plenty. There was no charge for anything here, of course.

Leaving Dupree's after dinner that cold day, about the eighteenth of December, we drove along the ridge overlooking Plum Creek and Cherry Creek Valley. A long string of Indians—afoot, in wagons, and some with travois—were moving toward Cheyenne City. We passed about a dozen sitting on the ground. Harvey said, "How," but there was no answer. On down the ridge we met some more. They were all stripped short on clothes, wearing breechclouts and leggins and decorated on top with paint and feathers. Some of them carried Winchesters and looked dangerous to an Iowa boy. One old skinny buck, Circle Lame, with his bowlegs and buffalo bow looked so funny that I had to laugh at him. He was in such a bad temper that he pulled out an arrow and set it in his bow. Straight Head stepped in front of him and said, *"Takesha"* ("wait"), and others growled, *"Wanetcha"* ("no"). But he pulled up on me anyway, and I thought I was a goner. Straight Head grabbed the bow and saved the day for me. The old codger likely wanted my scalp to add to his collection. I was glad to get down the trail so I couldn't hear the old man yelling at me.

Everything was all right at our store. The Indian police had watched it day and night. We put our horses in the back room and shut up everything while we got supper. It wasn't long before a hack came by with Lieutenant Hale from Fort Bennett and a boss farmer, John Holland, in it. From them we learned that Sitting Bull had been killed on December 15 and this bunch of two hundred Indians gathering there on the Cheyenne were stampeding from the Battle of Wounded Knee. The Indians had come 125 miles in about three days,

23

were tired, hungry, and scared. They made camp in Plum Creek bottom. Kindling was so scarce there the squaws had to go to the sand bars for driftwood. Having left in such a hurry, few had any bedding or food. It must have been a long, hard night for them.

The next morning we made a wash boiler of coffee, opened a box of hardtack, and took it down to them. Some of them came to the store and bought lard, canned meat, and sugar. About four o'clock in the afternoon, Captain Hurst came in a four-mule ambulance and had a lieutenant and two buck privates with him. After a long talk with the Indians, he made a deal with them. They were to surrender all guns and go to Fort Bennett to be fed until the trouble was over. That night all the able-bodied young bucks and some of the girls took the Winchesters and good horses and high-tailed it for the Bad Lands to join Big Foot's bunch. The next morning the old men filed by our wagon and piled in their war goods—clubs, bows and arrows, and even old flintlocks. I don't believe there was a usable gun in the whole wagon load. Captain Hurst made a deal with the Robinsons to furnish a team to haul the junk to Fort Bennett. He also bought a big steer from Angel, which was gone as soon as it was butchered. They were so starved they ate everything but the bones.

The next day I started for Fort Bennett with the wagon, followed by a two- or three-mile string of Indians. We stopped at Dupree's for the night. They killed a steer for supper and let the Indians bed down in the cottonwoods by the river. The Duprees were uneasy. After we went to bed, we heard a noise at the corral, and all the menfolks got up. When someone knocked at the door, Pete and Xavier got their guns, stood on each side of the door, and talking Indian sixty miles an hour, opened the puncheon door. In came a Fox Indian who worked for Narceese Narcelle, a half-breed rancher living over near Big Foot's camp. He had about twenty-five horses that he was taking over to the Rousseau ranch to remove a temptation from Big Foot. Both the Duprees and the Fox were scared and hardly went to sleep that night.

In the morning we went on toward the fort. A bunch of Indians with guns and on good horses followed on the opposite side of the river. By the time we got to Fort Bennett, they had dropped behind, and I was all alone. There I unloaded the guns in a warehouse, fed the team some U. S. hay and corn, had supper in what they called the messhouse, and bedded down in my wagon for the night. I tried to get my pay for hauling the guns, but they said it would be sent to the Robinsons later. So I started out with my tired team for home. The Duprees fixed me a lunch to take along when I went by there. That night I camped in a draw off from Robbs Flat and the big spring, far enough off to miss any Indian traffic along there. It was cold on the ground, but I got some sleep and was ready to get along early the next morning.

Everything was quiet at Cheyenne City. All the whites except the Robinsons and Angel were gone and only a few Indians were hanging around. In a day or two Charley took the team to Pierre, and I cut poles for corrals and put a couple of horses in it so we could skip pretty fast. It was Christmas time, but we did not feel like celebrating. Colonel Merriam came by with two or three hundred infantry and set up camp in Plum Creek bottom. The soldiers found a pile of posts left there by Little Bear's old cabin and dragged them to their Sibley tents to take off the chill. Just when the soldiers were ready to use them, an order was issued to take them back. Two four-mule teams then went out to scavenge for wood. Angel furnished hay for the horses and mules, and both stores sold a lot of things to eat. They had come fifty

miles in two days, and most of them had walked. Foot sol-
diering was hard in that country in those days.

All this time I had been working for the Robinsons for
one dollar a day when there was work. The next morning
I had a chance to improve my lot by hauling wood for the
soldiers at two dollars a day. They gave me a mean old
stampeder of a horse to ride as I guided about twenty men
with the two wagons up Plum Creek for dry wood. Fuel
was scarce everywhere in that country, especially around
Cheyenne. Little Bear's camp had been there, and they had
picked up all the dry wood within several miles. Being afraid
of ambush, the troops walked the bottom, and I rode the
ridge to serve as a lookout. The soldiers wanted me to use
an army saddle but I wouldn't do it on that cranky old horse.
He would get scared and run a mile every time I got on him.
The second time I rode him I put on a Mexican-made spade
bit, one of the cruelest bits there is, called a bear trap. One
of the lieutenants objected to this, but I went ahead anyway. With it I could stop the old outlaw and drag good-sized
poles to the wagons with a rope anchored to my saddle horn.
This was a good job about three hours every morning and
afternoon, but I felt sorry for the troops. Most of them had
had very little experience in the West, and both men and
officers were cold most of the time. Bundled up in buffalo
coats and leggins and running at the nose, they not only
looked helpless but had to keep moving to keep warm. Most
of the regulars were pretty poor sticks, being either city boys
or immigrants, and they were awfully afraid of the Indians
they had come to fight. They gambled a lot, drank anything
from lemon extract to whiskey, and spent the rest of the time
hauling firewood. There were very few officers left from
the earlier Indian campaigns, most of the present ones being
West Point graduates who had never experienced a South
Dakota winter. Though they looked helpless with their

runny noses and old-style heavy guns, this was the type of men who had given the Indians bad medicine at the Battle of Wounded Knee. I'll bet many of them learned that a Dakota campaign wasn't as romantic as they had expected it to be.

CHEYENNE CITY was not exactly a thriving place that winter of 1890–91, but it did have some troops there for a while, and one family moved into the settlement. William Harding and his wife had come to that country as soon as it was declared open for settlement and had built a cabin in a grove twenty miles from Cheyenne City. That winter they moved into one of Little Bear's cabins, and we all thought Mrs. Harding quite an addition to the "city."

One of the two traders there when I came in with the Robinsons was a fellow named Morris. When he drifted away, he left behind a big, white turkey gobbler. It would butt in when we fed the horses and was a general nuisance. One day I hit him a hard crack with a club and broke his neck. Harvey and I were alone at that time living on hardtack and salt pork, and the thought of roast turkey was a mighty pleasant one. We tried to pick him but the feathers were too tight. So we skinned him and dressed him the best we could, put him in a boiler, and sat up nearly all night keeping the fire going. By morning we still couldn't get a fork in him. We cooked him all morning and afternoon and decided to eat him that night even if he was tough as leather. It wasn't so bad, but we hauled what was left of that forty-pound bird down to the river and stuck it in the hole in the ice where we watered the horses.

When Morris came back, he accused Harding of stealing his turkey. We laughed about it until Harding came in and said he was going to kill Morris if he ever mentioned it again. The affair had gone far enough, we thought, so Harvey told

27

Morris that I had killed the bird. As the country was still under martial law, Morris made a complaint to Colonel Merriam, who sent a sergeant for me. I was sure scared. Harvey went along to act as my lawyer. The Colonel asked me to tell him all about it, then Harvey made a speech saying I was honest but didn't know much. This was partly true. Morris then made a speech that was fitting for an ex-lumberjack from Wisconsin, which he was. After the half-day trial was over, the Colonel said it was a very reprehensible deed and that he would take it under advisement until the following day. When we left, we could hear the Colonel and three or four officers laughing. Harvey said it would be all right. I went back the next day for the verdict. The Colonel said if I would promise not to kill any more turkeys, he would let me go. I promised all right as there were no more in the country. The Colonel then told me that he had been young once. I think he had a good time as it was very dull around the camp. The soldiers called me "Turkey" as long as they stayed there.

Since the troops had found a lot of dead cottonwoods and ash up Plum Creek, they didn't need me any longer as a guide. I bought a small stock of goods from the Robinsons and set up a store in one of Little Bear's cabins. I got along fair, selling tobacco, candy, and a few staples, and spending the nights with the Robinsons. One morning when I opened up I found my shelves cleaned out as slick as a whistle. Even my saddle was gone. This was quite a blow, for I had put in all my wages or about one hundred dollars.

I nosed around and found out that Buffalo, Angel's man, had gone and that he had passed Cavanaugh's store about twenty miles up the river carrying my saddle and a lot of other stuff on his back. I set out after him on my pony, left my big U. S. musket at Cavanaugh's since it was such a nuisance to carry, and went on to Big Foot's camp. There

I found Buffalo and Johnny Dunn had rounded up Big Foot's herd of about one hundred cattle and were trying to cut out about forty unbranded yearlings that weighed five hundred pounds or so. I watched them awhile as they tried to keep the calves away from their mothers, and then rode up on them. They started to run up the bottom, and I took after them. Getting close I shot over their heads and ordered them to stop. Even though both of them had big guns, they stopped and acted pretty scared. I told Buffalo he would have to go back with me and show me where he hid my store goods. He said they were in Angel's cellar. Fingering my Colt forty-five, I told him I would shoot him cold dead if he didn't come back with me. Both of them started back with me following, gun in hand. We stopped that night in an Indian cabin, where we found flour to make flapjacks with. I slept pretty light, but they did not bother any at all.

The next morning these renegades picked up two Ghost Dance shirts there in the cabin and put them on. The shirts were trimmed with fringe and decorated with pictures. Dressed up like Indians, they seemed to be in good humor with me. When we got near Cavanaugh's, they started their horses on a dead run and began to holler bloody murder. The Cavanaughs came out with their guns ready and were about to shoot me when they saw there was no danger. They were mad though, but did agree to give us breakfast for fifty cents apiece. It was getting dark when we got to Cheyenne City. Buffalo went into Angel's store and stayed a long time. Finally he came out and said the goods weren't in the cellar but were out in the big draw. He led me to the place and dug out the sacks. The next morning we started Buffalo and Dunn up the river for a long bareback ride, and I moved my stuff back into the ten-by-ten store. I had lost about twenty-five dollars on the deal, but I had shown two bastards that they couldn't fool with me.

CHAPTER 3

TAKING ROOT ON PLUM CREEK

THE CATTLE BUSINESS looked like a good one to me in
1891. Everybody you talked to was thinking about doing the same thing. It figured good on paper. Borrow money
at 10 per cent, buy a few cows, and the herd will double every
three years. Start with 100, three years later you have 200,
then 400, 800, 1,600, 3,200, 6,400, and so on. There was lots
of grass in that 11,000,000-acre pasture taken from the Sioux
in 1889, and there were very few settlers. Of course, it was
a hard life, with cold winters and hot summers, alkali water,
and danger of Indian uprisings, but it looked mighty good
to me.

30

I took up a claim on Plum Creek where there was a good spring, and from old Circle Lame, the chief whose legs were so bowed they made a good circle underneath him, I bought a five-dollar cabin that was on it. The Indians seemed to have given up the idea of Ghost Dancing and war and were moving back to their camps, rounding up their cattle, and settling down again. They still had to go to Fort Bennett once a month to draw beef and flour. This kept them on the road a good deal of the time. Some of the young men were being doctored the Indian way for their wounds received at the Battle of Wounded Knee, that is, by keeping the wounds open. It looked wrong to me, but I found out later that it worked. Anyway, they were now a defeated people and lived under the control of Uncle Sam's army and their own blue-uniformed policemen, who rode around a lot with their revolvers showing. The few old settlers came back in along with some new ones, all interested in cattle or horses.

The white ranchers were an average lot of people in most ways. They had to stand a lot of hardships such as droughts and blizzards. But all of them added to their herds by branding slicks. It was not considered stealing if one put his brand on young stock that were not following or suckling their mothers. Most people never bothered to eat their own beef. Since the bigger outfits swept away a lot of stock belonging to the little men at roundup time, it was proper for the little men to eat beef that carried a big outfit's brand. The attitude of a lot of big cattlemen was that the two-bit ranchers were a nuisance and ought to be pushed out of the way. In Johnson County, Wyoming, this led to a war, and the big operators brought in gunmen to do the job for them. The stock associations were dominated by the big stockmen, and they gave the men with small herds a rough deal.

I always got along well with the Indians who lived across the Cheyenne River. They were a lot better than some of the white men I got to know. If you went to their camps hungry, they would feed you their best jerked beef, bread, and coffee. Their style of eating was crude in manners but skillful in operation. With a knife they dug out a piece of meat, stuck one end in their mouth, cut off a good mouthful, then whetted the knife on the sole of a moccasin. If they got grease on their fingers, they rubbed it in their hair. The cutting of the meat looked dangerous as the knife came close to their long noses.

The women were patient workers but not good looking. At fifteen to twenty they were handsome, but they faded fast and soon became shapeless. Most of them were virtuous. Prostitutes were marked with a gunpowder tattoo dot in the middle of the forehead. The young girls were kept neat and clean and did very little work. The women cut and carried the wood, while the bucks hunted some, but mostly took it easy. The Indians had their good points all right.

Old Sitting Bull never gave up hating the whites. He said he would rather be a dead Indian than a live white man and classed all whites as liars, which was a pretty good guess. They took one old buck East to impress him with white man's superiority. When he came back he said the houses were about as high as the Black Hills, that whites were everywhere, some running one way and some another, and that there were so many he couldn't count them, but he guessed they were all crazy.

The old Sioux used to wrap their dead in blankets, place them up in trees or on scaffolds, and leave with them some things to take to the happy hunting ground. After the Indian agents came, they ordered burial in the ground, made the young bucks come into the agency to have their marriages legalized, and made long hair on a young man an illegal practice. These orders did not affect the old men. Little Bear kept his four wives—why, I never did know. There were some tree burial spots left when I went to Plum Creek. On my way to town I used to pass a body in a big cedar tree. A mouth organ had been left with it, and when the wind was in the right direction it would sound like it was being played.

These Indians could have survived pretty well after the government took them over if it had not been for white man's disease. The agency furnished oxen and plows and gave them fence for their gardens and patches of corn. All of them raised some potatoes and garden stuff as well as cattle and horses. But after they began to live in houses, T. B. came, along with the other diseases of white men—smallpox, trachoma, syphilis, and others—they died by the hundreds. In the bad year of 1900, whole families died of smallpox. The Indians set fire to the houses, burning bodies and all the contents. The half-breeds, mostly French, seemed to do better.

The old Lakotas were a good show, and I liked them. They knew when they were beat and took their defeat in good spirit. They had counted on the Ghost Shirt, but when they found out that it would not turn a bullet they knew they were gone. The new generation of Indians were not so good. They picked all the bad from both the whites and the Indians. It was from one of the old longhairs that I got my Indian nickname, *Minne Etka*, meaning drowned and come to life again. This was given when I was once reported drowned and the community had gathered to divide up my property when I came in on them.

The winter of 1890–91 was a tough one for both whites and Indians in Dakota. I had only cotton underwear and no way to get any woolens. I did trade for a big buffalo coat and got hold of a blue-gray army coat and a pair of cavalry boots. The boots were all right in the fall and spring, but in the winter one needed German knit sox, felt boots, and overshoes, none of which I had that first year. When the temperatures got down below zero, the Indians wrapped

33

their feet in jack-rabbit skins and then put on moccasins.
They refused to wear the U. S. Issue shoes as they were
nearly all too big and heavy for them. We could buy all these
shoes from them we wanted at fifteen cents a pair, I. D. Issue
coats for twenty-five cents, and blankets for a dollar. My
house was cold, but after I got my buffalo coat I could at
least sleep without freezing at night.

Most of the Indian stock was of no value to one setting
up in the horse or cattle business since most of it was scrubby
stuff. Indian ponies could be had at a price of ten to twenty-
five dollars. They had a few good American saddle horses at
fifty to seventy-five dollars. I bought one bald-faced roan
with stocking legs and a yearling colt for forty dollars. This
mare had belonged to old Circle Lame, and her range was
where I filed my claim. Since mares go to the same place to
foal unless they are herded or pastured elsewhere, Circle
Lame was glad to get the forty dollars for the two. I was now
in the stock business in a very small way.

My CLAIM was a lonesome place until I got used to it, being
about twenty miles from the nearest rancher. Howard and
Green were about twenty miles southwest, Harding about
that far west, Cavanaugh and Cheyenne City the same distance to the northwest. Pierre was ninety miles one way,
and the Sioux camps were strung across the Cheyenne River.
In June, 1891, I got my first close neighbor, but it didn't
help much if neighboring meant being sociable.

John Fleming camped about a mile up Plum Creek from
me and stayed there for four years. He was a mystery to me
and never did much to explain himself beyond saying that he
had been in Indian Territory, California, Idaho, and all over
the West. When he came to Plum Creek, he was about forty
years old, had a new wagon, a good roan cow pony and a
gray team, and over one hundred cattle, half being two-year-

34

old Minnesota steers and the rest yearlings. He was a first-class horseman and a good cook—that I learned as I rode with him over the years. From him I learned how to make good light bread and a lot of meanness that I would have been better off without having picked up. I had a feeling that he was revengeful and it was that which had got him in bad at other places and made him so suspicious of everybody. He acted as if he was always expecting someone to turn on him and never left his double-action Colt six-shooter and his forty-five-seventy rifle very far. After he left Plum Creek, he went to Idaho. I heard later that he had been sent to the pen at Boise for first-degree murder, and I can understand why this man with his suspicious nature and his gun scars got in bad. He was one of the few real bad men I ever met.

My claim was nothing but a piece of prairie when I moved out there from Cheyenne City with my wagon, my two ponies, a stove, and a few pots and pans. Near by were the two deserted Indian camps, each having about one hundred cabins and the one above me, Hump's, also having a pole and brush dance hall where the Ghost Dance had been held. I had bought a cabin from old Circle Lame and decided to move it. I took the logs down and marked each one, loaded them on my wagon, and hauled them to my claim. It took me about a day to take the cabin apart and move it and about a week to put it together again. Hay had to be cut to lay on top the roof poles, and dirt had to be thrown on top of them. I used an old pail for a stovepipe hole and chinked the logs with homemade mud. I didn't bother with a floor. From the Robinson store I got enough boxes for chairs and tables. This was the first house I ever owned, and I was pretty proud of it. Later I bought three other Indian cabins and used the logs for corrals. Using a rope and my little mare I dragged some cottonwood poles from the river and made a basket

35

rack for hay. After I got a mower and rake in Pierre that spring, I was ready to put up hay for wintering my saddle horses. In Hump's camp I found some traps, so I took a dozen home to use on wolves. As both of my ponies had been foaled on Plum Creek, I had no problem keeping track of them that winter and spring. Plum Creek was all right for drinking until the water got low, then it was alkali and made me sick. One day an old Indian came along and stayed for dinner. He said, "Water bad," and took me up a coulee to the west where we found a spring of cool, sweet water. After that I got two two-gallon jugs and carried water every day. Now and then, mostly then, I went there to wash my clothes and take a bath.

In my first winter on the Dakota prairie I learned how to camp out in the winter time. When I was working for the Robinsons and after I got out on my own, we made trips about twice a month to Pierre for goods. It was quite a job to keep from freezing on these trips of ninety miles. Walking along by the side of the wagon, picking up wood and cowchips for fuel, was about the only way, even though we had buffalo coats and blankets. At night we camped in a sheltered place among the ash groves, picketed the horses, and slept on the ground around a fire that we tried to keep going all night. Sometimes we could kill a little fresh meat along the way. On one trip I remember I fired my forty-four into a bunch of prairie chickens and got two, and farther on, I killed a badger. We skinned the badger but decided he was too fat to eat, so put him on the campfire and watched him burn in a bright white flame for about two hours. Then we pulled him out of the fire and had what was left for breakfast. These trips were tough on our noses, cheeks, and fingers. Oftentimes, they would burn and itch when we got into a warm room. Looking back on these trips, I wonder how we fared so well.

Pierre was a welcome sight when we came in off the frozen prairie. We headed for a livery stable where we put the team and then checked in at a hotel. A lot of cattlemen spent their winters in town, and they, with the soldiers coming and going to the Dakota forts, made business lively. It was booming in 1890–91. Horse-drawn streetcars ran up the hill to East Pierre where a big promoter had built the Wells House. The busiest place was the red-light district. It was always crowded with freighters, soldiers, and a lot of half-breeds. Only one or two houses catered to fullblood Sioux. Every saloon sold a lot of bad whiskey and Sioux Falls beer, and tin horn gamblers kept the faro and poker tables busy. In fact, saloons, livery stables, and the red-light district made up the biggest part of the business of the town.

When the South Dakota legislature was in session, I went to Pierre with the Robinsons. One of the boys had a brother-in-law who kept the Park Hotel, a swanky place, and we stayed there. Since they were paying the bill at two dollars a day, I went along. I did not like to be around all these well-dressed politicians and clean tablecloths after batching on the prairie in my own filth. I had quite a time learning to order meals. You were supposed to name every dish you wanted, but I got around that by telling the girls to bring me something to eat and a lot of it. The waitresses were imported from the big cities and were good lookers. Some were fast and some were slow, but all were well dressed and a sight to these lonesome Dakota bachelors. The hotel had bathrooms on every floor, and there were no rooms with private bath.

The legislature then in session was largely Scandinavian and American stock, and most of the legislators were pretty crude people. People around Pierre said that when the first trains arrived bringing in the politicians you could smell cow manure for several miles. Among them were some old-

37

time western characters. C. K. Howard, owner of the U+ Ranch west of Rapid City, was one of them. An old Civil War colonel by the name of Bullard, a very low talker, was another. Being agent for the North Western Railroad, he was opposed by Harry Hunter, known as "Old Two Sticks" since he carried two canes, who was a lobbyist for the Milwaukee Road. Bullard kept the capitol at Pierre through two removal fights.

It wasn't easy to leave the politicians, the pimps, and the pretty girls of Pierre and go back to my dirt-floored eight-by-sixteen shack on Plum Creek and live on my own cooking and with my own company most of the time. But once back to what a man called home, it wasn't a bad place to be. Now and then in the evenings, I would hum to myself "Golden Slippers" or "Dan McGinty," or make the sod roof shake with

> Oh, the chickens they grow tall in Cheyenne, in Cheyenne,
> And they eat them guts and all in Cheyenne, in Cheyenne.
> Oh, the women wear the britches in Cheyenne,
> Yes, the women wear the britches in Cheyenne.
> Oh, the men are sons of bitches in Cheyenne, in Cheyenne,
> Yes, they're dirty sons of bitches in Cheyenne, in Cheyenne.

AFTER a dull summer of putting up hay, I decided to buy some cattle and see if they would use the multiplication tables for me. I wrote to Pa back in Winfield, and he said he would lend me some money. He told me that one of our old Winfield neighbors who now had a livery barn in O'Neill, Nebraska, would buy up a few cows for me, and I could go down there to get them.

About August 1, I set out for Nebraska, riding one horse and leading another. The first night I stayed with A. C. Van Metre where the town of Van Metre is now. He was a fine, generous old man who had lived in Dakota for forty years, had a half-breed wife, and had sent his children away to school. The next day I made the forks of the White River and stayed with an old Indian woman and her kids. After picketing my horses, she fixed me a bed on the floor with some quilts and served me alone since Sioux women do not eat with men. When I left the following day, she gave me some biscuits to take along. Below the White River breaks, I saw no one or any sign that anything except deer and antelope lived there until I hit an Indian camp of about twenty cabins that evening. There was no one at home so I helped myself to some roasting ears and potatoes from their patches and filled up good that night. For breakfast and dinner the next day, I had warmed-up roasting ears and spuds again. I stayed at a pretty good half-breed's ranch on the Keyapaha River that night. They could not talk much English, but they had plenty of good grub, and I was tired of corn. After bedding me down for the night, they loaded themselves into a hack and went to a dance down river. I ate breakfast with them when they got back in the morning, and headed southeast again. None of these people living in the grass country made any charge for food and lodging. All of them seemed friendly and glad to have a stranger come by.

At Springview, Nebraska, that night I put my horses in a feed barn and holed-up at a small hotel. This country was settled by homesteaders, a lot of them being foreigners. The soil was sandy, and there had not been much rain for several years, so everybody was awful poor. The homesteaders would haul in a load of hay with their ox-teams and sell it for one dollar to the livery barns. Since I had about eighty miles to go and my horses were getting footsore, I stayed over a day here to get a real bath in a tub, a shave and a haircut, and a new shirt and a hat. The hotelkeeper was old and his wife was young. The second night she wanted me to take her to church, but the old man objected. While they had a squabble, I went to the pool hall and stayed until they had gone to bed. I didn't want to be shot in such a God-for-saken place as Springview.

After eating dinner with a homesteader for a half-dollar the next day, I got to Bassett where the sheriff held me up. There had been a lot of horse-stealing around there. The vigilantes had killed one man lodged in jail at Springview and had hanged several others. Some said horse-stealing was then at a low ebb in those parts. After telling the sheriff I knew some people at O'Neill and that I was going to buy some cattle, he let me go, but I think he still thought horses would be safer around there if he had taken me down to the cottonwoods and strung me up.

At noon the next day I was in the Irish settlement named after the Fenian, John O'Neill. It was a wide open town and pretty rough. The settlers were hard up, but the Wyoming cowboys and gamblers kept the red-light district and the saloons booming. I went to the Star Livery Barn where I bought twenty cows and six calves, paying $400 which I had borrowed, and set out for the William Griffiths', old family friends, who lived north of there twenty miles.

It was late when I got to the Griffiths'. They helped me pen the cattle, and then we had supper and talked until very late. At one time they had heard that I had drowned and later that I had been killed by the Indians. Fearing for my life, they urged me to settle north of the Niobrara River which had been opened following the Sioux surrender, but I was not interested. In the four days I was there, we branded the cattle with △ on the left side, after which I had no fear of a sheriff or bunch of vigilantes along the way. There weren't many eight-by-ten shacks between there and Plum Creek, but I felt better with a bill of sale in my pocket and a brand on the cattle.

40

At the Niobrara the steers balked and acted like they had never seen water before. Four Indian boys rode their ponies across to help me. I led a gentle cow across and her calf followed. The boys drove the rest over and we all got across in good shape. When I gave the Indians two sacks of Bull Durham and papers for cigarets, they were so pleased they went along with me for four or five miles. At noon that day I stopped at a wild plum patch and ate a lot of them. That night I penned my cattle at Spencer, a new town of shacks and small stores, and slept in the hotel. I spent the next night with an old homesteader who had more than his share of bedbugs. This was the last of the partly settled country. I followed an old Indian trail northwest through a good grass country and got to Bonesteel where I spent the night with Jack Sully, who had been in the country for years. He had an Indian wife, a son, and a hired man, and was putting up hay for winter feed when I ran across him. I found him very pleasant and intelligent, and he refused to take any pay for my staying with him. We ate beef that night, but not from his herd.

I hit the Missouri at the old Rosebud Landing where steamboats took on wood and unloaded freight for the Indian agency eighty miles west. There were a few old log buildings left, and a half-breed and his family lived there, though the Rosebud agency had been abandoned. He had some crops as well as horses and cattle, and his house was neat and the food good. That night he played his fiddle and sang some tunes in poor English. When I left he refused to take any money, so I gave him some Bull Durham which seemed welcome.

Until I got to White River the next evening, I never saw a soul. A family of fullbloods lived there, had a garden and a cornfield and a small herd of cattle and ponies. For my food and lodging the man said I could give the woman twen-

41

ty-five cents as she wanted to buy a comb. A quarter and
two sacks of tobacco pleased them very much. After cross-
ing the river, I followed the Chamberlain-Black Hills trail
and met two ox-teams of German Mennonites, or Russians
as they were called, going east to Chamberlain, which was
the end of the Milwaukee Railroad at that time. One talked
English and told me they had a colony on Medicine Creek
twenty-five miles northwest.

When I got up at daybreak the next morning thirteen
cows and calves were gone. I herded the rest of them north
to a settler's place and had a boy there watch them while I
went back to follow their tracks south from my camp. I
found them standing in the White River willows and spent
the day getting them north to where I had left the rest of the
herd. The next morning a calf was gone, so I went south
again and found the critter lying there in my old camp waiting for its mother. When separated, cows and calves go back
to the place where the calf sucked last. Now I had the whole
bunch together again, but my horse had a big swelling on its
withers and was pretty well worn out. I traded him to a
Russian settler for a sorrel mare. She was quiet to lead and
saddle but when I got on her she reared up and fell back. I
worked all day with her and found that by leaving the
cinches loose and not pulling on the bit she went all right.
I spent another night with the settlers, paid the boy one dollar
for herding my cattle two days and the same to the woman
for my food. Money was pretty scarce among all new
settlers and this looked big to them. I had learned the hard
way that cattle will not stay put at night unless there is water
and grass around. After that I didn't try any dry camps
with a bunch of cows.

Here I was at the Medicine Creek Russian colony sixty
miles from Pierre and 150 miles from my log mansion on
Plum Creek. There were no ranches between the settlements,

and I had a badly spoiled, unbroke mare and twenty-six big and little cattle worth $400. Being my first venture, these cows seemed to me as valuable as all the gold in the Black Hills. From one of the Russians I got two loaves of bread and a dozen hard-boiled eggs for a quarter and started out. The mare did not want to leave her old haunts and would rear and fall back, so I had to lead her or risk being killed or crippled out in this no man's land. In the first two days I ate the bread and eggs, and the next day I lived on plums. Fort Pierre looked good to me that afternoon at four. I turned the cattle loose in a grassy spot, put my nag in a feed barn, and after a double order of beefsteak I felt better.

There did not seem to be any loafing place around except saloons, so I went into a joint behind a false front. It was a dirty place lined with loafers sitting on beer kegs. I told the tough-looking bartender that I wanted a glass of beer. While he fiddled around drawing it from a keg, one of the bar flies come up, friendly like, asked me how things were in the country. I tasted the beer. It was warm. The bartender asked my "friend" what he wanted, and he said whiskey sour. Four others lined up at the bar. He took their order. They watched me. I knew I was getting the works so I laid a silver dollar on the bar. He looked at me rather hard, said it was $1.60. The first bar fly asked me for a loan of two dollars, said he felt lucky and wanted to try the monte game in the back part. I wanted to get out of the place so I slid another dollar across the bar. The bartender put it in the till and looked out the window, rather bored it seemed to me. I saw it was my play and said, "How about the change?" He looked out into the street, walked slowly to the till and got the change, and laid it on the back of the bar near the back room entrance. I started out pretty mad. He called out, "Get your change." I told him, "Keep it. You need it worse than I do." Their mouths flopped open, but no one made a

43

move. Saloons then and now are good places to keep out of.

I went across the street to a store and bought four cans of tomatoes and some other lunch stuff, put it in a sack, went to the barn for my nag, and rode out of town. I drove the cattle up Bad River about three miles and while they stood in the water, I had a bath and washed my clothes. That night as I lay on some buffalo grass trying to sleep I cussed my "friends" at the saloon in Fort Pierre. I was out two dollars but had got a lot of experience. The rounders in Fort Pierre were always willing to divide, that is, take half of all one would give them. There were a few good people in Fort Pierre. Some argued there were fifteen or eighteen, but others said that estimate was too high.

After a breakfast of sardines, crackers, and coffee, I decided to go across the Missouri to Pierre. The cattle had filled up and were lying in the cottonwoods, so I rode into Fort Pierre and was rowed across in a skiff for twenty-five cents. At the post office I found two letters from Pa and Ma, so I sat down right away and told them about my cattle. Pa had loaned me the money to start in the cattle business, and I wanted him to know that all was going well.

Going from Pierre to Plum Creek, I got tired of sardines and tomatoes but had no trouble with the cattle. The first night I stayed at a road ranch, the only one on the way home. I left the cows at a water hole and went in for a good supper. The bed looked fair but was so full of bedbugs that I finally went out to the barn and slept on the hay. After that I slept on buffalo grass and covered myself with an old comfort. At Robinson's store I got some grub and pushed on home. I found everything all right in the cabin, but cattle had pretty well cleaned up the feed outside. The next day I raided the Indian preacher's garden on the big flat and got a sack full of corn and potatoes. I was now ready to settle down to the life of a rancher and watch the herd grow. One can pass away a good many hours by just watching the calves play and the cows fill themselves with grass.

CHAPTER 4

THE UPS AND DOWNS OF CATTLE RANCHING

THE BIG pasture west of the Missouri that the Sioux had turned over to Uncle Sam had few ranchers in it when I went there in 1890, but within another year or so there were all kinds of livestock roaming over it. The cattle were of all kinds. My Nebraska cows were mostly Shorthorn and were big and fat. My neighbor Fleming had what we called Minnesota dogies, a mixed bunch of dairy and scrub stock. Scattered around us were dehorned Longhorns, and other stuff. A. D. Marriot of Pierre had brought in 2,000 pure Longhorns from West Texas, and Fleming and I had helped put the Topped Hat brand on them. They were a wild, mean bunch, and all the little ranchers would cut them out of their herds and chase them twenty or thirty miles just to get them out of sight. There were also a lot of Hash Knife, Turkey Track, and other brands scattered around my place.

The big outfits did not like the little ranchers, and the little men did not like the big ones. Between the two there was a lot of bad blood over who could claim the range that neither of them owned. A lot of them had no idea of right or wrong, and the newly organized Stanley County officials didn't look around much to see if they could find trouble. The little fellow never thought of killing one of his own steers for beef but always picked on a brand belonging to some big outfit or a neighbor who lived quite a way off. In that part of South Dakota a lot of cattle were butchered in lonely little draws, and only a black spot on the prairie marked the place where the hide was burned. The law of the range required one to hang the hide of any critter killed on the corral fence so anybody could see the brand, but that was done only in the case when you killed your own cow. When you steal—this wasn't called stealing, of course—you sure don't want to hang the evidence out on the line.

One day in January, 1892, I rode to the Deep Creek breaks where my cattle ranged and found nothing but a lot of empty space and a dim trail leading southwest left by the hooves of my cows and a couple of horses. With tears in my eyes and a Colt in my hand, I followed the trail for twenty miles or so before coming home with a tired horse. There had been reports of an outlaw pair on the head of Bad River, and most people were afraid of them. I thought this must be the outfit that I was after. I went over to Fleming to see what he thought I ought to do. He had heard the outlaws had been to Marrington's ranch and stayed there when only Hank Randall was at home. Fleming set out for Pierre to see

47

what the grapevine would have to say about my cattle, and when he came back he reported that they had been driven to the mouth of Grindstone Creek on Bad River. There the outlaws had changed my △ brand to A, and had moved the cattle into the Bad Lands to the west. Everybody seemed to know all about it. The newspaper and radio of that day was the grubline rider and others going back and forth. I suppose everybody hanging around the saloons of Rapid City or Hot Springs knew who stole my cattle before I did. Among the drunken cowboys of that time, the rustlers who stole from a timid Iowa boy who did not gamble or drink were popular. I was just outclassed, that's all.

There was more than cattle at stake, so I rigged up a bedroll and a cook outfit and started toward the Bad Lands. In a couple of days I went through Cedar Pass on the old Indian trail and found a campsite off the road. There was a seep of water from a spring for my horses to drink, but I had to melt snow for my coffee. Sage hens and rabbits were plentiful so I had meat to eat. I turned one horse loose to graze and picketed the other to a tree.

This country had been called Bad Lands by the Indians, and the whites had counted it no good. It seemed desolate and lonely as I started to look over the place. There were a lot of old camps, mostly Indian, with rusty cans and other junk around. Bones were all over. Long jaw bones with big teeth looked like they were petrified. Buffalo horns were old and ready to go back to nothing. Elk horns were still solid. Small herds of antelope and mountain sheep, all pretty shy, were around. Coyotes and big gray lobo wolves were all over. Cattle and horses were plentiful in most places. Some of the horses had saddle and harness marks on them. Most of all, there was just lots of scenery, a kind of a jungle of land, and one could get lost easy if you did not spot trails and landmarks as you went along. The first settler in the Bad Lands

48

was a man named Schweinhart, but his name is no longer remembered there. The branded horses and cattle I saw there in 1892 belonged to Messingale and Ross, a big outfit which headquartered on White River.

After roaming around there for a week, I gave up my cattle as lost and headed back. I still had hope of finding some of them in the spring roundups, but I had a better idea as to how to get back into the cattle business again. In the Bad Lands I had seen thousands of head of livestock, some of them not branded, or "slicks" as we called them, and I had made up my mind to get my share. On the way back I went through Midland and stopped in the hotel to get cleaned up and fed up again. I was still pretty wooly from camping out the last two weeks, had a red nose and enough beard to look bad. The other guests were a nosey bunch and wanted to know where I had been and where I was going. It was not a pleasant stop, but the cooking was good. After eating, I bought bacon, canned milk, coffee, and crackers, and re-packed my bedroll and cooking utensils. The stuff was sure a mess. The Midland loafers looked on rather scornful at this pack, which even I knew looked bad. When I was rigged up and ready to go, one of them asked which way I was going. I told him straight up and rode north on the old Spotted Tail Trail.

When I got home and got a sort of a bath, a shave, and had something to eat besides bacon and crackers, I went over to tell Fleming about all this unbranded stuff I had seen in the Bad Lands. Being an old maverick hunter, he was interested and wanted to go right away to round up a bunch of them. He said people would talk about us for branding slicks but that it was legal since in the range country the man that got his brand on first was the owner. The cattle round-ups would start in May, and the big outfits would get all the slicks unless we acted, and if we didn't burn our brands too

49

deep they would heal before long anyway. Horse owners did not have regular roundups but hunted them in an independent way, mostly by two or three riders going at it to capture a few good horses by cornering them in a canyon and slapping a brand on them so they could claim them later. The row about slicks was an everlasting one in the whole western country, but the main lot of horse and cattle ranchers did not like the hard riding which it took to brand them.

I had made up my mind. My thirty-one cattle were gone. There was no workable law to protect me in my losses. Though I was scared of the deal, I had decided to get even. Fleming and I bought a light wagon from the Indians, U. S. Issue not to be sold, and rigged up a small mess box with cooking kettles, dutch oven, bedding, and ropes. Fleming threw in his old Winchester for good measure.

One February day we started out, wrapped up in buffalo coats and felt boots and trailed by our two saddle horses. We stayed at the Midland Hotel the first night where we had good meals and a good night's rest in the bunkhouse. Fleming played poker with three of the loafers and lost twelve dollars before he got in a row with them. We bought a lot of grub, including a four-dollar gallon jug of whiskey, and struck out for the Bad Lands the next morning in zero weather. Two and one-half days later, after chopping through sixteen-inch ice to water the horses and nearly freezing on the open prairie, we were in the center of the Bad Lands. There we found a cottonwood grove in the loop of a creek with twenty-foot cut banks all the way around, and set up camp in the neck of it. We had a roll of wire so fenced in the loop. This made a good pasture for our horses and anything else we could catch. For two days we scouted around this strange country. There were deep creeks and draws impossible to cross, and mountains and hills so rough that a horse couldn't get over them. The horses we found

A herd of beef near Fort Pierre

were pretty snorty at first, but we got them to camp all right. While we were there, we rode them a lot to save ours. We found one bunch of sixteen tame gray horses with no brands on them, led by an old white mare with harness marks on her. There was one full-grown stallion in the bunch, but he didn't cause any trouble. We drove them into the canyon, made a rough catch pen out of ash poles fastened to trees, and put a dim brand on their left hips.

There were a lot of wild horses everywhere, but we didn't try to catch any. Wild broncs are a spoiled lot anyway and hard to gentle. Besides the ground was frozen and the patches of ice made it dangerous to ride hard, as one had to do to corner them. I got one bad fall anyway when the sorrel mare I had got from the Russians started to make a turn on ice and fell flat on her side. I fell on both hands and wrists, and they were so sore and lame I could hardly use them. Anyway, we decided to get out of there with the gray bunch and call it a day.

While I stayed at camp, Fleming scouted for a trail out that had a corral where we could pen the horses at night. Going north across a flat prairie, he came to Peno Springs, the old stage station, where Mexican Ed ran a road ranch. He arranged for horse feed at $2.00 a day and grub for ourselves at $1.50, and came back to our camp. First, we took our wagon and camp traps out north of the Bad Lands and went back the next day after our horses. We caught the old mare and led her along, and the others followed. That night we had to make a cold camp short of Peno Springs. It was a job cutting a hole in the ice for water. The old mare was hobbled and our horses were picketed so they did not wander off in the night. We got on our way early in the morning.

At Mexican Ed's we penned our stock and had a good feed of plain ranch grub. After I had washed up and didn't look quite so wooly, I went to sleep in the room with four double bunks while Fleming and Ed sat in the kitchen and played cards. These two rooms were the living quarters in one corner of the big stage barn. Ed cooked supper that night, making light bread and a pie. He was an awful good cook. Fleming brought in what was left of our gallon of whiskey, and he and Ed got pretty noisy before the evening was over. The next morning they had such a bust head that I had to feed the stock and cook breakfast. They said I was such a poor cook that they wouldn't eat any of my cooking but did drink some vinegar and water. Both lay in their beds and swore off drinking forever. It stormed all day, and no travelers came by, which was a good thing considering the condition of Ed. That night, even if they weren't feeling so good, they started playing poker again, after Ed found another quart of whiskey somewhere.

After this spree was over three days later, Fleming and I caught some of our slicks and trimmed their manes and tails which made them look more like farm stock. While Ed and Fleming went to old Smithville thirty miles west to get grub, I hauled some wood and cooked some fifty-cent meals for travelers. A few stayed all night but most of them were in a hurry to get to Rapid City. When Fleming and Ed came back, they had two fellows with them to look at our horses. We sold all the new ones except the old mare for $40 apiece, and were paid on the spot in five-, ten-, and twenty-dollar gold pieces. By spending two weeks and around $50 for supplies, we had made $600. I hadn't quite recovered my $400 loss on cows, but I had made a good beginning.

Mexican Ed wanted us to stay all winter with him free, said he hadn't had such a good drunk for a long time. He wasn't a bad man. A few years later he was shot and I served on the jury that sent his murderer to the pen for fourteen years. Fleming later went to prison for first degree murder. It may be a good thing that we decided to get on home.

Going east on the Black Hills–Fort Pierre Trail, we turned the old white mare loose, and as she trotted away toward the Bad Lands, we wished her luck. That night we stayed at Grizzly Shouns' Road Ranch, where we had good food and beds but not the spree. The next day we got to Louis Green's on Plum Creek. Fleming told him we had been to Deadwood and busted the faro bank. We made him promise to keep it a secret. To make the big tale stick good we gave Louis' wife a five-dollar gold piece. Louis wanted the details so he could try it when he shipped cattle that fall, and Fleming sure poured it on for him. Going around the country telling big tales was one of the standard jokes of South Dakota. If you could get people to believe them, you were considered pretty smart.

We got back to my cabin before sundown the next day and found everything all right. Fleming cooked us a good meal while I fed our jaded horses. It had been a long hard trip in February weather, and I was glad to be home. We had over $250 apiece for the work, but we had earned every cent of it. Hunting horses could be interesting, but it is tough in the winter.

I SAID earlier that I learned several tricks and some meanness from Fleming. I could also add that I got back into the cattle business because he wanted to get out of it. He thought the small rancher was in a poor position with his cattle scattered to hell and gone and the big outfits driving them farther when they swept through the country at roundup time. He said he wanted to go into the sheep business, buy some dogs to herd them and to chase cattle, eat other people's beef three meals a day, and get even with a lot of men he didn't like and a lot who didn't like him. This feeling of revenge was a good break for me, but it may not have been for a lot of the big outfits.

53

Sometime in February a Pinkerton detective, Tom Horn, came to see Fleming. There was trouble in Johnson County, Wyoming, and the Pinkertons had been called in by the big ranchers to rid the range they had used for years of all settlers and rustlers. Horn offered Fleming $150 a month and expenses to go to Wyoming to help, and a bonus of $500 for every rustler killed. The $500 was prorated if there was more than one man at the killing. This cost the big cattlemen a lot of money and most of them went broke. Hiring killers to get rid of outlaws was not even considered right by most people, let alone killing little ranchers who had the law on their side. Horn stayed around for some time trying to interest Fleming in this chance to make a good living. He bought some whiskey, and they had a celebration that lasted a week. Fleming furnished the meat by killing a Black Angus heifer belonging to some big brand, and they brought me a hind quarter. It was extra good. But after all the arguing and celebrating Fleming refused to take the job, said his cattle were scattered over all South Dakota and he couldn't round them up in six years let alone six weeks, and besides he wanted to go into the sheep business and really make life unpleasant for the big cattlemen. Horn went on without him, and I heard ten years later that he went to the penitentiary for murdering a small boy. Fleming must have gone to prison at about the same time. They were a pair of dandies if I ever saw one.

When Fleming offered to sell me his 116 Minnesota dogies for $2,000, I was interested even if they were scattered everywhere. I wrote Pa down in Iowa about the loss of my cows and told him about this chance to buy Fleming's brand, taking everything I could find. He sent me the $2,000, and getting a bill of sale, I started riding the Plum Creek country to find what I had bought.

In the spring of 1892, a Hash Knife outfit had a wagon

and a roundup outfit working the White Thunder bottom and the Plum Creek country. It was but a part of the big Hash Knife roundup that had five or six other wagons operating in Montana, Wyoming, and South Dakota. This wagon, as a roundup crew was called, had a boss, a cook, forty to fifty men, and from four to five hundred saddle horses from several different ranches. I joined them for a few days while they were in my parts to see if I could protect the unbranded yearlings among the cows I had bought. It was quite a sight to see them work the cattle, and I guess I made quite a nuisance of myself. I would go to the chuck wagon and eat dinner but rode home every night. In the day I stayed near the bunch of local cattle they cut out to see if I could see any of my own.

These cowhands were mostly old-time horsemen and were expert ropers and good broncbusters. When the day's catch was milling around, the men on the cutting horses could drop a rope on any pair of horns and drag the critter over to the branding fire or turn it out into the separate bunches where the different brands were held. One afternoon I saw one of the hands ride a green bronc. It was an extra good buckskin wearing the Hash Knife brand. The man had a fancy hackamore made of calfskin with a noseband of rawhide and a neck piece and lead rope of different colored, twisted horsehair. There was no bit in the mouth. The rider had a little help getting the hackamore on and a blindfold over the bronc's eyes. A saddle was put on and the blind pulled off. The horse bucked around a ring the length of the lead rope held by the broncbuster, who was still on the ground. After that, he blindfolded the horse while he got on, then pulled the blindfold off and let him go. The animal bucked long and hard, and the rider rode easy, quite loose from the waist up. It was really an artistic job, by both the horse and the man. After the horse quit pitching, the

55

rider gave him a lesson in starting, stopping, and turning. Then he got off, rolled a cigaret, and blew smoke rings. It was all in a day's work. The cattle roundup crews did not ordinarily stop to catch and break range horses. That was done at another time. The Hash Knife outfit had one of the best bunches of horses on the range since they turned Thoroughbred stallions loose with their bronc mares. When they saw an extra-good one at cattle roundup time they had missed earlier, they just dropped a loop over his neck and added him to the saddle stuff they carried along.

It takes a tough man to stand the work of a roundup. The hands are up at daybreak and have breakfast before it really gets light. Everyone rolls his own tarpaulin, quilts, and blankets into a tight roll and loads it on the bed wagon. The cook and volunteer help wash the dishes while the four horses used on the bed wagon and the four for the chuck wagon are brought around and harnessed. The riders saddle up and some start taking the rough edges off their broncs, which have to do some unlimbering every morning before settling down for the day. The cook climbs on his wagon, the night hawk on the bed wagon, and the day wrangler gathers his stock at the rear. The boss details one man to pilot the outfit on to the next camp ground. The boss does not get on his horse until the wagons are on the move and likely does not say a word. When he gets on, that is the signal that the riding has started for the day. The cowhands follow the boss to a hill on a stiff lope, and he sends ten men this way, six that way, and so on. He has to know his country well or he would lose the outfit every day. While the boss makes his way with the wagons and loose stock to the next camp eight or ten miles away, the circle riders begin their sweeps. All will meet by night at the next camp where the sorting of the different brands takes place.

After the pilot gets his outfit to the camp ground, one

wrangler keeps the horses away from the cook's water hole. The pilot and the other wrangler then unharness the horses, leaving the collars, harness, and bridles where the wagons stopped. Two of them start on a lope to find some dry wood while the cook begins his fire with what little wood he has in the wagon. In a pretty good time the men are back, dragging wood at the end of their ropes. It is everybody's job to keep the water buckets filled, plenty of wood handy, and help the cook wash dishes, as he is a very busy man getting meals for fifty men or more. There is meat to cook, bread to make, dried fruit to soak, beans to bake, and other things to fix that taste awful good to hungry men. If the cook wants beef, he orders it, and they pick out a fat two- or three-year-old heifer, shoot her near the wagon, butcher her on the hide, and hang up to cure what is not cooked fresh.

Before the boss and some of the riders come in with some of the cattle, the pilot and the wranglers have made a rope corral for the saddle stock at some distance from the chuck wagon so the dust will not blow on the food. The space for fifty feet around the cook is holy ground and the cook is the Almighty. If things go wrong, he will raise hell. Maybe he will anyway. He is the only one who can cuss not only the hands but the boss, too.

All this time the day herders are bringing the herd along slow-like behind the saddle horses. These cattle are the ones being moved to another range and are herded day and night. Day herders go on duty as soon as they eat breakfast, and it is a tedious, poky job but easier than riding the long circle. Some days they may not move, and the herders can sit in the saddle on a little knoll and take it easy. One may take a nap while the others ride around the herd. While the bunch is bedded down at night, they take a two-hour turn every other night. Day herding was not a popular job.

When the morning circle is done, the cattle are bunched

and two hands from each ranch taking part in the roundup are sent in. They cut out the stuff carrying their brands, and the rest of the bunch are held apart since they either belong on that range or are unclaimed. They will be turned loose after the calves have been branded. The cattle wearing the brands of the other outfits, called the "cut," are put in the day herd after the calves have been branded and castrated, and carried along with the roundup. This is a complicated business, and a man has to know his way around or he will get lost in the shuffle. The best rule is to follow the boss, say little, and keep your eyes open. It isn't very romantic—just a lot of dust and hard work.

All of this I saw for the first time in the spring of 1892. I spent a few days with the Hash Knife wagon to see that they didn't get any of my cattle in their big day herd. If mine got in that big herd of 4,000 to 5,000, I would have to follow along and wait until they worked the big herd later. Some of the Plum Creek ranchers had to go fifty miles northwest to be there when the roundup crews cut the strays out of the herd. That was not done until they made the first slicing off of the brands belonging on that range. The small cattlemen were at a disadvantage in this, but some of them stuck it out and got most of their stock.

One of my steers got in one of these herds and went into a throwback bunch and finally wound up in Wyoming, where the Stock Association shipped it to Chicago and the money went into their stray account. I could never get them to let me have it even though I showed them the proof that I owned all cattle carrying that brand. A few years later when I was in Chicago with a load of cattle, I went in to see old Clay Robinson about it. He told me I would have to bring a lawsuit to get it, and I told him I would collect on the range anyway I could. He did not like it and talked pretty mean to me. The Wyoming Stock Association accumulated a lot of money in the stray account this way. I never heard of a little rancher getting any pay for the cows he lost in these big roundups. I think the big outfits lost more than they gained this way. Their cattle were scattered all over the range, and no one watched them except at roundup time. We little men had a lot of good eating as we evened things up, and a lot of people in that country didn't even need that excuse. The big ones kept imposing on the little ones as long as I lived in that country, and the overstocked ranges and the bad winters of 1886–87 and 1896–97 helped even up matters quite a bit.

It's an ill wind that blows nobody good. Maybe, if my cattle had never been stolen by those outlaws, it might have taken me years to plunge in deep enough to buy over 100 head at a crack. Maybe, if I had not gone to the Bad Lands with Fleming, I might not have been around him when he sold his herd. Anyway, I was in the cattle business in 1892, and already I had learned that there was more to it than turning cattle loose on government land while I sat back and watched them double in number every year.

The Plum Creek country began to settle up in 1892. By fall there were enough neighbors around to take off some of the lonesomeness of living on the prairie. It helped just to see another human now and then. Most of the new ones had about as many children as they had cows, but it was the cattle that put the pressure on the range and made it harder to keep track of the bovine property we owned.

An old Texan by the name of Painter moved in on Plum Creek that spring and lived in a tent with his young wife and eight kids. He was a carpenter and was kept pretty busy building cabins around the country. His hired man, Shoemaker, who roomed and boarded with the family, took a shine to Painter's pretty wife. One day when the whole

59

family was on the way to Pierre, the old man hiked off the trail to look for a water hole while the others waited. When he got back, the wagon, wife, hired man, and kids were gone. He followed the tracks awhile, then turned back home to see if they had circled around there. But no family. The neighbors helped him look, but nobody ever found them. For a time he was pretty much put out but finally came out of it. He said an old man like him had no business marrying a young woman in the first place, said he couldn't do justice to her, and that it was an unequal contest from the beginning. Some of the neighbors thought Painter got a bad deal, but he allowed the kids would eat Shoemaker into the poor house and the woman would drain all the sap out of him in no time. Finally, the old man left for Texas, and that was the last we ever saw of him.

Another new settler was Dr. Kennedy, a doctor for an insurance company in Illinois, who had read how cattle double every three years so was out there to make his fortune fast. In fact, if it would have worked the way he thought it did, there would not have been room on the whole earth for his cattle inside of a few years. It turned cold while he was at my place so we spent a lot of time reading the books he brought along. When he criticized my housekeeping and cooking, I brought out the old rule on him and made him do the cooking while I did the outside chores. After about a week he admitted he was worse than I had been.

When warm weather came, we went to Hump's old camp, where there was a good spring and plenty of cedars in the canyon. Kennedy got a pretty good cabin built, with a floor and windows, and moved his family out. The one hundred or so mixed cattle that he bought got scattered so far he never did find them. The bank foreclosed on the mortgage but never recovered much besides the cabin. Then he hired out at forty dollars a month to herd sheep. In the big blizzard of 1896 he froze to death, and only 200 of the 1,500 sheep he was tending lived through. His family hung on for a while, living on little more than what the cat brought in, and then disappeared completely.

Down at the mouth of Plum Creek, South Dakota Blair moved in with about two hundred cattle and a small bunch of horses in the spring of 1892. He was an extra-good horse man. One of his broncs had a wire cut on the front foot. He had tried to doctor it and had got the horse to fighting him. It would strike, bite, and kick, and made a man wonder if the Pearly Gates were open in case he got on the receiving end. Blair wanted me to ride the bronc when he got well, thinking I could gentle him down a bit. I was afraid of the animal but the offer of five dollars to take a good ride looked too tempting. After I rode him all forenoon, the horse still showed a lot of fight. Blair wanted me to keep going, so I stayed in the saddle till night. The horse was all in by then, but he still bit and kicked when Blair got near him. I was so all in that I had to crawl off on the corral fence. The next morning Blair came up to my place in a lather wanting his five dollars back, saying that the horse was dead and I had killed him. This kind of a neighbor wasn't a lot of help when we little men were trying to stand together against the big operators. But sheepman Fleming was always there. He dogged the cattle and cussed his help, but he was a good neighbor to me.

Over on Morphadite Creek, Buck Williams moved in with about two hundred cattle, which he ran north in the open country. He was an old trail driver and had made his first trip up from Texas in 1878. By hook and by crook he had got together a fair kind of mixed cattle and at last had started out on his own. His first camp was a tent which he moved in haying time down creek to the rough breaks. Then he and his help made a ten-by-twelve dugout by laying log

61

walls up three feet and digging out about three feet of dirt underneath. The wheat grass, sometimes called alkali grass, was two or three feet tall where he built and the water was bad, but flies, mosquitoes, and rattlesnakes did right well there. I went to see him in July. He had run out of grub and had killed a badger to live on. Buck said the meat was as good as possum, but it had a rank smell and taste. He had "pahboiled" it, he said, not having brought up any *r*'s from Texas with him, but still it stunk. I had dinner with the old coot and can say that if you ever want a cathartic, laxative, purgative, cramps, and gripes, all at once, just drink coffee made of alkali water and eat "pahboiled" badger.

Old Buck was going to start a roundup after haying and wanted me to come along. I had two mares to ride. He said they would be a nuisance but to come anyway and night wrangle the saddle stock. The rest of them would pick up my cattle and would furnish me a couple of old saddle horses when I needed them. This was all right with me, as I would learn more about the roundup business and would get some of my cows home.

I kept a lookout for the time to start, and in about ten days I got word to come to Robbs Spring on the flat between Deep and Morphadite creeks. When I got there, I found quite a collection of people. Mexican Ed was the cook. Tex Hamphill, an old Texan, had been elected boss. Johnny Robb, whose place we were met at, was to go along. Then there was Bill Hurst, George Holly, and Raymond Herbert, or "Abear" as we called him since he was a Frenchy. As soon as I got on the scene, they began to kid me about the mare, wanted to know if she were stump broke and to show me where I would picket her at night. In the morning they all said I had lied and that the mare was not stump broke. This mare joke was standard all over the range country, but it embarrassed me no end. I saw the point that bringing a mare to a roundup was a bad social error. Mares and stallions are not allowed, and there are plenty of good reasons for the custom. I saw that I had to get a string of geldings if I wanted to get in even the small roundups again.

The first day I rode the mare and watched the roundup they had made that morning before I got there. They had a herd of mixed stuff, mostly Minnesota dogies that were dehorned and wearing a collection of brands. There were some Circle D Longhorns belonging to the Duprees that were pretty good. The cows weighed over 1,200 pounds and the four- or five-year-old steers would run up to 1,400. A few old outlaws that had outrun the Dupree boys in other roundups were also in the net. They would weigh from 1,600 to 1,800 pounds and had a horn spread of eight to ten feet. All of the Longhorns were about the same color since old Fred wouldn't use any bull but a buckskin and blue critter. These big mean-looking cattle made some of our dairy stock look pretty small.

In the herd that afternoon was one big buckskin cow that was hard to cut out. All the old hands tried their best but couldn't make it. Johnny Robb, Mexican Ed, and I held the bunch and the rest of the hands ganged up and finally got her in the bunch that was turned loose. She looked ten feet high and could trot a gait that outran our best horses in dead heat. They cussed her as she took off. This was fun for me, for the old cowhands are a conceited lot and I was glad to see them trimmed down to size by a brindle cow.

After letting Robb's cattle loose and sending Buck Williams' stuff home to Morphadite Creek with one of his men, we crossed the Cheyenne River to go to Abear Creek. I rode my mare and drove the sixty-five saddle horses. Abear acted as pilot to show Mexican Ed where to go with the chuck wagon. The rest rode in a bunch off to one side. They should have driven the loose saddle stock since I was night wrangler

63

and was not supposed to do anything in the daytime but help the cook. But they knew I was green and timid and gave me a raw deal. That night we camped at Abear's little cabin and pole corral after a twenty-five-mile move. I was tired and my nag was all in. I couldn't get any sleep myself, but I did get another horse to ride that night. After the saddle stock spooked and I had to run them two miles to turn them, I put them in a tight bunch and held them there until morning. It was wrong to keep them from grazing all night, I knew, but since the roundup crew had been smart to me I decided to be smart to them. I had adopted a policy of treating people good if they were good to me and if they weren't, give them back what they sent. That might not be very Christian, but it worked on both the horses and people I lived with in South Dakota.

The next morning the gang made a circle west to Dupree Creek and brought in five hundred cattle, mostly Dupree's, but also a lot of unbranded older stock. Dupree claimed they were his, but since there were a lot of stray brands that nobody recognized we did not pay any attention to him. A small bunch of Robb's, mine, and a few others that belonged south of the river was cut out and penned. About five hundred were in the circle after the next morning's run, and again they cut out the cows belonging south of the river, which included some of mine.

The roundup broke up the following morning, and Robb and I started out early with our little herd. It was foggy, and we could not take any bearings. At noon we found ourselves back at Abear's camp, having wandered in a circle all morning. After eating a box of lunch Mexican Ed had sent with us, we started out again, following the wagon tracks we had made coming over. That night when we camped Robb and I were so sore at each other that we wouldn't speak. We were tired and cross without any supper or breakfast. When we could see the Cheyenne breaks the next morning, we knew we were going the right direction. At noon we got to Doug Carlin's place, where we had a good, warming dinner, and then on to Robb's place that night. I penned my cattle there and spent the night with him. He was a neat housekeeper and a good cook but not a very good prairie man. He was too old to learn.

It was only twelve miles home, so I made that easy the next day with my thirteen cows. I caught a fresh horse and went to the spring to take a bath and get some good water. It was good to be home again. Not long afterward I saw old Fred Dupree. He blamed my roundup crew for the loss of his blue Longhorn bull. I never saw all that went in the bunch that the fellows took on north from Abear's place, so could not say for certain that he wasn't right. However, I knew that he had branded a lot of slicks in his lifetime and even if we did take a bull, he was still way ahead.

After I had finished my haying, I heard that Marrington had started a small roundup south of Bad River. I decided to horn in on it to see if I could find some more of my $2,000 worth of cattle. Riding a two-year-old gelding colt to improve my social standing, I went down below the Black Hills–Fort Pierre Trail and found them on Mitchell Creek. It was a small outfit, the Marringtons—Fred, Lester, Artie, and Elton—Hank Randall, and Buck Williams. I told them I would help but had nothing to ride but my colt. They said for me to join them and ride one of theirs. It was my job to ride the day herd since they penned at night. For two days I kept going on my gelding, but when he got so tired he could hardly go, I decided to ride their horse, which I knew must be an outlaw. I stayed on him the first time I tried and took a big circle. Then I got off to tighten a cinch. In getting on again I was careless, and he pitched me over his head. It did not hurt me, so while one of the men snubbed

65

him to his saddle horn, I got on again and everything was all right from then on.

After working Frozen Man and Plum creeks, Marrington turned back. I went home with Buck and turned eight of my steers in with his. We didn't work very hard and monkeyed around quite a bit. Hank's piles bothered him and he went to Midland one day to get some medicine. When he came back the next day, he was pretty drunk and had forgot to get his remedy for piles. Instead he brought a gallon of whiskey. We laid off all day and about everybody got soused. The roundup was over anyway by that time, so after branding a few calves for Buck, I went back to my cabin, taking my cows along.

I was getting low on cash and in need of a few things, so I decided to ship twenty of my critters. After three days spent looking at the back end of a cow, I penned them in Pierre, ordered feed for them, and went to a restaurant for a good meal. The next day after I cleaned up some and bought some new clothes with my fifty-dollar advance, I moved the cattle down to Jim Lighton's Ferry and crossed the Missouri to the loading pens. Later I got a draft for the first stock I ever sold. They averaged 1,090 pounds in Chicago, and after the freight and commission were taken out, I had $560. That price wouldn't let anyone get rich very fast, but it was a mighty comforting feeling to have some cash in my pockets for the first time. I had also learned that if you want to make friends, you don't ride a mare at roundup time.

CHAPTER 5

HIGH JINKS ON THE PRAIRIES

IN THE FALL and winter of 1892–93 I was about ready to pull out of Plum Creek for good and start up somewhere else. Everybody seemed on the outs with everybody else, and it wasn't all because some of us lived on O. P. (other people's) brand beef. If it hadn't been for a love affair and the problem of finding my cows, I probably would have looked for greener pastures.

Sheepmen and cattlemen never did get along. Here on Plum Creek there were several little operators who had sheep. They would dog the cattle, and their blatting sheep would eat the grass right down to the roots and stink up every water hole for miles around. My neighbor, Fleming, had gone into sheep and was always having trouble with his sheepherders and other people's cattle. He would dog the cows and run them clean off the range he tried to claim for his own. His herders were always quitting and coming over to my house to gang around a few days. Since it was harder to get a sheepherder than a cowhand, he was up against it a lot of the time and blamed me for his troubles with his men.

That winter two men, Elton Marrington and Frank Lampe, mysteriously disappeared and no trace of them was ever found. Blame was placed on several people and a lot of clues were followed, but no bodies were ever found and the grapevine never seemed to know much about it. Usually, when a man was killed in that country, the grubline boys knew all about it and passed the word along pretty quick. This was a blank mystery then and still is.

On the way to Pierre one day I saw a man trailing a bunch of horses east. He had been on the road all summer coming from the Idaho country. The horses were Oregon cayuses and were wild and mean. I bought a four-year-old and a seven-year-old from him and hired an Indian by the name of Widow to help me break them. I rode the old horse. He did not buck at first but would go along quiet like for a long way and then turn sideways right quick, give two or three bucks, and then run for dear life. I could never go to sleep in the saddle on that animal for over six months for fear I might have to walk ten or fifteen miles and maybe even lose a horse and saddle forever. With these two horses and my two mares I was on the way to getting some geldings so I could follow the roundups.

One morning out on the flat by my place I found sixteen extra-good stray geldings, a mix of Thoroughbred and Morgan stock, wearing the Horse Head brand on the left hip.

I penned them and fed them some of my hay for three or four days. When Cavanaugh came by from Fort Pierre, he told me this bunch had stampeded at night from a road ranch twenty miles west of Fort Pierre and that a reward was offered for their return. Riding one that had saddle marks on it, I started out with this wild and spooky bunch on the fifty-eight-mile trek to find the owner. They galloped or ran the first thirty-five miles and trotted the rest of the way. We got to the road ranch inside of four hours, and the horses were gaunt and wet with sweat. I found out they belonged to a red-headed Scotchman, Sandy Agnew, from over near Rapid City. The old man came out with his one blue eye and his one black eye flashing and dressed me down for running his horses that way. He said I ought to have my hind-end kicked but instead gave me a twenty-dollar reward for bringing them back to him. I found out later that he had offered the best horse in the bunch as a reward. This little bunch was just a part of a bigger one that was being moved east from Elk Creek to market, and all of them had trouble with stampedes. Finally, they all went back where they started from and started all over again.

When I got tired of cutting ash and cedar posts that winter, and that was pretty often, I visited around quite a bit where I could pick up a meal or two and talk to someone. One of the most interesting trips that I made several times was up to the Cherry Creek subagency to see the Indians get their monthly ration issue from the government. About all of the villages had moved north across the Cheyenne. Hump's camp of about one hundred houses was empty on the big flat near Kennedy's Spring. Old Circle Lame had left twenty or so houses and a frame schoolhouse behind at the forks of Plum Creek. Only Little Bear and his four wives, living in three log houses and a canvas tepee, stayed behind. On ration day all of the Indians in that neck of the woods

69

moved in on the agency with their dogs and ponies, and it was quite a show.

I suppose life was pretty dull for most of these Indians, and the trip after food was a big event. They started gathering about a week before the issue day and spent their time gambling, horse-racing, and just visiting. There were always a few half-civilized white men there to sell liquor to these wild savages in spite of the law against it. Most of these people were hungry, having nothing left but flour, and some of them didn't have that. On the big day, the Indian police climbed into the corrals with their big revolvers and began killing the sixty or seventy Texas steers inside. They shot them through the heart from the side, not in the head as white men do. When they got the cattle down, the boss farmer divided them and teams dragged the carcasses out to the various villages. Then the women took over and did the butchering. In about an hour everybody was eating fresh beef and cooking more. This went on all day and most of the night.

The issue of clothing, called *wakpominy*, was made only now and then. The Indians did not like the clothing and would not wear it if they could swap it for something else or could make their own. I don't believe I ever saw an Indian wear the *wakpominy* shoes that were so big and heavy. They didn't like the other stuff either. The feel of a moccasin made of cow hides or antelope skin was what they were used to, so they sold their shoes for fifteen cents, coats and pants for a quarter, and blankets for a dollar to anyone who was there to buy. It would have been pretty hard on us South Dakota pioneers if we could not have bought this stuff from them. The agency did its best to protect the Indian from the whites, wouldn't let them sell their cattle or horses—branded ID for Indian Department—without a permit, and kept an eye on the booze peddlers. But it was a pretty hard job to do.

70

I SPENT quite a bit of time that winter down at Little Bear's camp near Cheyenne City. He had been allowed to keep his four wives, and they lived with him in the three cabins and a canvas tepee. Little Bear was quite free with his ration-day meat, which he jerked by cutting it with the grain in thin slices and drying it. When it was all gone, he would come to my place to eat and talk. Since the Indians' guns had been taken away from them after the Battle of Wounded Knee in 1890, they couldn't get any wild stuff except what they caught in traps. That meant they were short on food before the next monthly issue was made. Old Little Bear did like to eat. After he had filled up, he would lean back and say, "How, how," meaning good.

Living with Little Bear and his menagerie was his grand-daughter, Chantay. She was a pretty sixteen-year-old, and since she was the only girl in that country, I thought she was pretty nice. The four grandmas kept her dressed in fancy clothes, waited on her hand and foot, and watched her pretty close when I was around. She had been to the Indian school at Pierre and had learned some English, but since the teacher was a strict and cross old maid, she said she did not want to go back. The Indian kids called this teacher "Old Pain in the Face," and when she heard of it she was crosser than ever. I kept going to Little Bear's place to see Chantay but could not get her to talk much when the old women were around. She would pull her shawl up over her head, leaving only one eye uncovered, and answer all questions, "I don't know." One day I met her alone at the store, and she said to me, "You see that hill." I told her I did after looking across the creek. Then she told me to meet her there when it got dark that night, to bring a blanket, and we could talk. It was there that I learned the beginning of how to make love to an Indian girl.

71

I was there early, and she came trotting as soon as it was dusk. She was dressed in calico, wore moccasins, and had her hair in braids. When she got started talking, she was a chatterbox. I just listened. She talked a lot about how she hated to go back to school because of "Old Pain in the Face" and a man called "Stud Horse." This man had a way of crawling in bed with the girls at night and had left several of them pregnant. She said she wanted shoes and stockings and a white dress like the ones the girls in Pierre had. She wanted to live in a house that was made of boards and painted white, with beds, tablecloths, and white dishes. Sometime she wanted to ride on a train the way the white people do, but she was afraid to. She wished her skin was white and that she had a real mother instead of her bossy grandmothers. She knew right from wrong, she said, and before long she would marry a good Indian boy if he had a spring wagon with a top on it to ride in on Issue Day.

Once I took a big Norwegian with me to visit Little Bear. He took a shine to Chantay and asked her in English if she wouldn't go to bed with him sometime. The four squaws seemed to understand enough English to know what he said and began to yell in Sioux, "Bad, bad, leave fast, leave fast." He started for the open prairie like a wild bronc, the women close behind. As he got on his horse, one picked up a big bone and hit him in the back of the head with it, knocking him off. Little Bear stopped the fracas, and the Norwegian high-tailed it out of there. I never saw him around there again.

I kept going to see Chantay three or four times a week after I had broke the ice that night and learned how to court Indian-style. At our hide-out she would sit there and crack gum. She said she got two sticks on ration day once a month. I got her both chewing gum and gum drops, and she was well pleased with me. She would put a whole package of gum in her mouth at once and chew like a goat. The rest of the candy and gum was taken home, where Little Bear and the grandmothers ate it up without stopping. The old folks were so well pleased with me that they let her come see me any time she wanted to come.

Chantay was touchy. Her limit as we sat under the blanket was to hold hands. But she was an everlasting talker, mixing English and Indian in a way that I could not understand all of it. At times she was gay and happy, at others dissatisfied with everything. Usually, she talked of white man's things that she wanted. She had just enough mission religion on top of her Indian beliefs to be mixed up. She thought she would likely go to Hell and meet me there sometime as she was so wicked. But she had a good number of old four-letter words that she used on anybody she didn't like, and she felt no wrong in using them.

The Robinsons' wives teased me about the candy and chewing gum I bought at their store and about my prospect of being a squaw man. When I went into the store, they would ask how much gum I wanted this time even when I had no idea of getting any. I would blush and then blush again because I was blushing. Then they would ask me, why not buy it wholesale? It was fun for them but it nearly got me. I decided to quit going in there for candy. The next time I was in Pierre I made a deal at a wholesale house to buy me a bucket of gum drops and a lot of chewing gum. I intended to fool these teasers, but when I got back home I found that the police had been through picking up Indian kids and had taken Chantay back to school. I took my bucket of candy home and hid it until I had a chance to trade it to some Indians. That year when some of the children ran away from school and tramped eighty miles home, Chantay sent word for me to bring an extra horse with me to Pierre and help her get away. But I decided to leave well enough alone

73

and never saw her again. I heard that she married a big buck a year or two later and soon faded into a plain Indian. Little Bear moved across the Cheyenne River, and I saw him now and then on Issue Day. He would say, "How, how," and I would give him a sack of Bull Durham. This he would mix with kinnikinnick to stretch it out, and would be very pleased about it all. I guess I was pretty lucky about the whole deal.

BEFORE the South Dakota winter closed in on us, it was the practice to go into Pierre and get enough grub to last most of the winter. I did this in October and dug a hole in my cabin's dirt floor and put the stuff in it. An old quilt covered it. As long as one was around and had a fire, it didn't freeze. We made no sheds for the livestock but did put up some hay-stacks to help get them through the winter.

Sometime that winter Cavanaugh, the former Boston stevedore, sent word to me that sixteen of my steers had strayed up to his place on the Cheyenne River, where he had a store and a few cattle, and he wanted me to come get them. I got Hank Randall, who was holding down Marrington's ranch while he spent the winter in Pierre, to go with me. It was a cold day's ride, and when we got there we spent most of the night thawing out on Cavanaugh's whiskey. An awful argument over religion was started that night by Hank with Cavanaugh. It looked like there would be a fight at first, then they would take a drink and shake hands. In a little while, they would start insulting each other again, and then they would fill up the glasses and shake hands again. Hank was quite a barroom singer, and his favorite was a ditty about the life of a sporting lady that ended, "Lulu was an old favorite, a good time was had by all."

The next morning the whiskey had died in us, but we were awful sick. In that five-hour ride home in sub-zero weather, we suffered pains, cramps, and all the misery of a hang-over. When we got to my cabin, we penned the cattle and made some coffee. Hank went on home to feed and water some stock he had in the corrals. He asked me to come over the next day to see if he were dead or not. I went over in the morning, and he told me I looked like hell. I said I felt that way, too. That night we doctored with vinegar and soda, and both swore off from ever drinking anything stronger than alkali water again. It lasted until the next time for both of us, though I was never much of a drinker. Hank thought some fresh beef in order after our appetites came back, so we went out and killed one of Henry Angel's fat heifers. We burned the brand part of the hide and Hank took the rest of it to make a lariat. I took a quarter home with me. Later, Henry wanted Hank to show him the hide as the range law required. All Hank had to show was the lariat. Henry blamed both of us for the loss of his heifer, but we knew he was eating beef, too, and that it probably carried the O. P. brand. It was a case of the pot calling the kettle black.

I had a yen to go back to the Bad Lands to get some more horses but did not want to go alone. Hank couldn't go since he had to feed a few old cows and calves for Marrington. He advised me not to go alone as he knew that range was taken by Missouri John of Wyoming. This was a pretty tough out-fit and would either run me off or kill me. I decided to go anyway, so got my camping stuff together and started. I stayed at Louis Green's the first night. He thought I was going back to Deadwood to break the faro bank and said I shouldn't go without Fleming. The second night I stayed at Grindstone Butte Road Ranch and the third night at Mike Quinn's place. I told them I was going to the Bad Lands to look for a new location for a ranch. They said the range was already taken and couldn't take any more stock. All I would

75

find there was trouble. I could see that they were on Missouri John's side. To throw them off, I started backtracking until I got out of sight, then turned and entered the Bad Lands through the Big Foot Pass.

It was no trouble to find the place where Fleming and I had camped the winter before. A pile of our firewood and an old ax were still there. I chopped a hole in the ice to water my two horses and made a cold camp. The next morning I took my slowest horse to look around. There were a lot of Missouri John's horses scattered all over. I found one bunch of slicks that had two nice yearlings in it, and the next day I got on my sorrel mare and tried to chase them into my trap there in the bend where I had my camp. They drove easy until I got within a mile of the place, then a little white mare with red ears turned off on a ridge and led the bunch in some broken country. I wound up ten miles from camp with a played-out horse. The mare staggered and acted like she would fall. She would hold her head down, shake it, and scatter sweat all over me. I let her drink, but the alkali water only made her feel worse. I was ashamed for having run a good horse this way when there wasn't a chance. It takes an awful good horse carrying a rider to outrun a wild bunch. So I made up my mind to quit and go home. I walked all the way back to camp, picketed the two horses, and cooked some coffee, bacon, and flapjacks before I went to bed. I knew the project had failed.

When I woke up and looked for my horses the next morning, they were gone. The ropes had been cut, and there were tracks of a man and a horse in the snow. I got breakfast quick and started on the trail but never saw hide nor hair of them. When I got back cold and tired, someone had been there and burned my saddle and bed. Here I was afoot one hundred miles from home and the world looked pretty blue. If I hadn't stored some of my grub and an extra U. S. blanket in a little cave, I would have froze to death that night. But I curled up in that cave and found myself alive in the morning.

The next morning I moved my camp to a little pocket about a mile toward White River. It had a washout cave so I could be a little more protected. There was wood but no water except melted snow. I still had enough grub to last a few days and had my thirty-two Smith and Wesson revolver and twenty cartridges that I could use to kill some rabbits. The sensible thing for me to do, I knew, was to get out of there by foot as fast as I could, but it was awful to think what all the people would say about me when it got around that I had walked home. I could tramp seventy-five miles south across the Pine Ridge Reservation and maybe get on the train east from there, but my feet were already blistered and frostbit. Besides it was risky for a white to be seen alone on the reservation since some of the Indians still had bad hearts. If I ever did get home, I knew I would sell out as quick as I could and go back to Iowa and get a job inside. I always wanted an easy job where I could wear good clothes and get bleached out. I was a sick bird.

The rest of that day I rested up, doctored my feet with snow, and mourned over my bad luck. The next day I packed my grub, pots, and blankets into a roll and was ready to go when I looked over my brush screen and saw a rider about one hundred feet away. I recognized him as Bill Newsom, the head of a cattle-stealing crowd that operated on the White and Bad rivers. This was the outfit that stole my Nebraska herd. He had a Winchester and a belt gun that looked like a forty-five Colt. It looked bad to me, so I kept my head down and watched. He went a little way, got off and tied his horse to a tree, took his Winchester out of the scabbard, and started looking around close like he was hunting for tracks. He moved slow-like toward my old camp. I

77

was pretty sure he was looking for me and would take a pot shot at me if he had a chance. When he got a quarter-mile up the trail I took my roll, made a run for his horse, and got on fast. The horse was snorty and wild but I stayed with him and laid on the leather. Inside of two hours I was across White River and the scare had worn off some. I cooked the best I could and at the same time kept an eye open for any other riders. That night I found an empty dugout and stayed there. I cut through two feet of ice to get water, which I warmed, and washed my face for the first time in several days. There was grub there so I had biscuits, bacon, coffee, and that night I had my first good sleep in several nights.

As I went southeast the next morning I came to a sign that said "Nebraska," and a notice not to trespass on the Pine Ridge Reservation, but I acted like I couldn't read. About four o'clock I was in the little town of Merriman on the railroad. Wanting to get rid of the horse and saddle, I went to the stockyard and put him in the pen and fed him some hay. Then I went to an eating place and filled up. After dark I went back to the stockyard, took the saddle off of the old bronc with the worked-over brand, and turned him loose. He snorted a few times and beat it across the prairie. I hid the saddle in an empty boxcar, threw the rope away, and took my pack up to the depot. There I bought a ticket to Valentine, Nebraska, and rode the caboose of the first train out that night.

After a few hours' sleep in a Valentine hotel that looked as tough as I did, I got up early to buy some new clothes so I could change my appearance. Seeing a suit in a window marked eighteen dollars, I went in to look it over. A squirty-looking young fellow was just sweeping out. I told him I wanted a suit like that one in the window. He looked at me and said that the suit was eighteen dollars, like that was about all the money there was in the world. Of course, I knew I looked like a bum in my dirty Indian-issue outfit and with a month's growth of hair and whiskers, but I sure didn't like his attitude at all. Pretty soon the boss came in. I took four twenty-dollar gold pieces out of my pocket and jingled them a bit. This made the clerk come to life all at once. The boss told him to go on with his sweeping, and he took personal charge of my case. After some haggling, he let me have the tweedy-looking suit for fifteen dollars, and then I bought a shirt, underwear, shoes and cap. I changed right there, leaving most of my *wakpominy* stuff, and bought a canvas telescope case to ship my boots, blanket, and cook stuff to Pierre in. When I left, I told the clerk he could have all the old clothes I left behind.

At the barbershop where I got a bath, shave, and a haircut, I filled the ginks hanging around there with a lot of baloney. They wanted to know where I came from and what I was doing. I told them I had been herding sheep in Wyoming about two years and had saved up $1,000. Any man with $100 in cash in Nebraska in 1893 would rate as a millionaire now. To make my story better, I told them a man couldn't herd sheep longer than two years and not go batty, so I was on my way out for a breather. It went over pretty well.

The next morning I got on an early train to Omaha. It was well filled with people, mostly poorly dressed. There were also a few well-dressed salesmen who tried to occupy two double seats with their feet and bags across from where they sat. Once in a while someone with courage would break up one of the deals and get some sour looks and rude remarks. The candy butcher peddled peanuts and other things. He tried to sell me a pretty interesting-looking book filled with pictures of naked women. When I refused to pay $1.50 for it, he was sore as a boil.

Omaha seemed an awful big place to me after living on

79

the prairies. There was a big noise at the station where the drivers of the hearse cabs and buses kept yelling about the various hotels. I found my way on foot to Farnham Street to a restaurant I had been in back in 1890. I asked the waiter about a room, and he sent me to a little hotel where rooms rented for one dollar a day. The place was equipped with what they called a water closet having running water and a lavatory. The bathroom was separate and kept locked. For twenty-five cents you could get it opened for you and a couple of towels were furnished. These things were pretty much of a mystery to most country folks, and they would forget to flush the water closet, which caused trouble.

I was not in a hurry to get back to Plum Creek so I stayed in Omaha awhile. That night I went to a theater. The "Nigger heaven" seats cost ten cents, those in the balcony twenty, and the lower floor or dress circle were thirty. I tried the ten-cent seats first but gave it up as too tough and a rowdy place. The show was a bunch of vaudeville acts, dancing, singing, and acrobats. One comedian would whack another across the rear-end and the crowd would clap their hands and stomp their feet. There were also a lot of old gags, some of which are still in use by the top comedians of our day. I went to the stock company shows the next few nights, seeing *East Lynne*, *The Silver King*, and *Rip Van Winkle*. There were big crowds and everybody seemed to have a good time.

Omaha was the first big town I had ever been in, and it was a sight for a country boy. There were a lot of well-dressed people everywhere, carriages pulled by fine horses, and all kinds of amusement. In the six days I was there I got so I could refuse a panhandler and not pick up the ones who tried to make friends with me. Before I left I understood the water closet, the gas light in my room, and the bathtub. I saw a lot of pretty bright men start down the line at night, get drunk, and wind up without their money or watches. Of course, it was their fault, as they should have said their prayers and gone to bed early. A sucker is born every minute, but they were there in swarms. I shouldn't talk much about it, as I have bought a lot of high-priced experience in my time.

I left Omaha on a slow train for Sioux City, where I had to wait for the train running to Hawarden. While I was in the depot, a nice-looking girl asked me what time it was. I told her. Then we began to talk. She invited me to go home with her. When I said I had to catch a train, she wanted me to go a piece with her. When we went outside, she said let the train go to hell. Coming from such a pretty girl, this set me back. She told me she "could do the Landershuffle and if it ain't good mamma will sift for you." I began to catch on and turned back. She wanted me to give her a quarter for luck, which I did, and she said, "Good-bye, baby."

While I was waiting for the North Western train at Huron, I met Ben Ash, who had given me my first job. I told him about my troubles in the Black Hills. He seemed amused and told me I had better stay away from both the Black Hills and the Pierre saloons until it was quieted down. He didn't think there was any danger of the law being after me and the best thing for me to do was to keep my mouth shut. This made me feel better and not at all afraid to get back home. I was a wiser young man when I crawled between my own blankets out on Plum Creek a few days later for the first time in nearly a month.

CHAPTER 6

TWO WORLDS–RANCHING OR RESPECTABILITY

BEFORE I could leave Pierre to go back to my sagebrush claim, I had to buy or borrow a horse. While I was looking around, I ran across a cowpuncher called Happy Jack who had spent his summer's wages and was homesick for dear old Arkansas. He offered to sell his outfit, and I bought the whole shebang—a big bay horse, a good saddle, bedroll, and a Colt six-shooter with a flashy ivory handle—all for $100. Before I pulled out of town, I went into Fletcher's Drug Store to get some salve for my sore feet. There were a few loafers around and one of them asked me where I was

82

headed for. When I told him I was on the way to the Bad Lands to look for stolen cattle, I realized that one of them was Bill Newsom himself. He looked at me and I was plenty scared, but I noticed he turned white and nervous. That made me feel better as he had quite a reputation as a gunman. He didn't say a word and neither did I. It was just a looking contest. As I went out the door I swaggered some to make sure he got a good look at the flashy six-shooter hanging from my belt. I was young and timid in some ways but quite a hand to stick up for myself in dealing with these bad ones. I found if I stayed out of the saloons I was about even with them. Ninety-nine per cent of all the toughness was a bluff anyway, and even killers don't want to get hurt. I never saw Newsom again, but I heard that he was later a sheriff in Cody, Wyoming.

Going home, I stopped at Fred Fruh's the first night and played muggins with him until I was so sleepy I couldn't see the spots on the dominoes. At Charley Foster's the next night I learned that he had heard of my Bad Lands affair. I had a good dinner of beef, biscuits, spuds, and coffee the next day at noon at old Fred Dupree's. Travelers just rode up there, put their horses in his corral, and stayed as long as they wanted to. Once in a while men would come from the East and stay there for several months. It didn't seem to be any trouble to feed another one or two when there were thirty or forty in that French-and-Indian family to feed every day. Besides, he had 4,000 Longhorns and 2,000 horses running loose, and I suppose a lot of people besides guests lived off of his beef or rode his horses. When old Fred died in 1898, he had $25,000 in gold under his bed. It wasn't long before all the cattle and horses were gone and all the buildings and corrals deserted.

When I got to Plum Creek at last, I found everything all right. The cabin was only eight-by-eighteen and had a dirt floor, but it was home. The next morning I found my two horses that I had last looked at when I picketed them at my Bad Lands camp. The sorrel was still thin but was picking up. After I had looked around, I went over to see Hank Randall. He asked me what in the hell I had been doing? I showed him my new six-shooter and told him a lot of big tales. He allowed as how Bill Newsom would get me some day.

All of the Indians around had just received a payment for the land they surrendered to the whites, and these silver dollars were burning a hole in their wampum bags. These dollars were about all that circulated in that country, though we did have five- and ten-dollar bills. One young Indian came to me and wanted to buy my big bay horse. I sold him for sixty-five dollars and he paid me in silver, which just about weighted me down.

In the middle of the winter the Robinsons wanted me to drive a team to Pierre for them to get a load of goods for their store. It took me three cold days to get there by way of Dupree's, Foster's, and Fruh's. When I got back to Dupree's a few days later, there was a crowd of Indians and whites gathered there for a big dance. Old Fred took me to his house, and we drank a lot of his wild-grape wine. As we drank, Fred described the dance then going on in one of the buildings: "My boy Pete, he play de fid. Xavier, he play de bull fid. Armyn, he dance, the sona bitch." When we went over to the cookhouse, the square dance was on. The tables and benches had been taken out to make room for two sets. There were a lot of capers and hopping around. I thought some of the girls were very well dressed. I tried dancing with some of them and got along fair. Old Fred had a loud voice and made a lot of noise. I noticed I was talking and laughing a good bit and was a little dizzy after guzzling so much wine. Pete and Xavier called it over at four in the morning. Quilts and blankets were brought out and everybody went to sleep. The next morning I got my horses sorted out of the crowded corral and went on my way. It had been a wonderful trip to Pierre.

A few days later a man from Minneapolis, Minnesota, by the name of Fred Burdick, came by my place. He was going into the sheep business and wanted to buy my claim. I had only a squatter's right to 160 acres and it had a pole fence around it. When he offered me $300 for the claim, my three ponies, an old wagon, and my hay, I took him up on the condition that I could stay until spring. I got along good with him and his nice-looking wife and two-year-old daughter until I pulled out.

In April I left for A. D. Marriot's ranch on Morphadite Creek to help in the roundup. I had seen him in Pierre when I came back from my Omaha trip, and he had propositioned me. His 2,500 cattle were scattered all the way from Pierre to Rapid City on the bottoms of the Cheyenne, White, and Bad rivers. If I would help hold the herd during the round-up, he offered to bring in any of my cattle they found. This sounded like a cheap way to get some of my scattered stuff rounded up for shipment, and I might find some of the Ne-braska cows that Bill Newsom had stolen and taken to Bad River.

We spent the first week of May gentling about fifty of Marriot's horses for the roundup saddle string. The different wagons moved to their positions that week. Bill Welch took his outfit to Fort Pierre, where he was to start from. U+ Jack took his wagon east and south of Rapid City a few miles. A Black Hills rider called Farting Elsie rode off to join Hol-combe's OHO wagon on the Belle Fourche. I went with Jack most of a day to help him drive the herd of fresh-broke horses, then came back to Marriot's, where Bendrickson and I were to hold all herds brought in to us. We had about twenty new horses there at the ranch that we had to watch pretty close since they had been bought at different places.

It wasn't more than two or three days until Bendrickson and I had our hands full. Welch sent in the first bunch of 300 or 400 Longhorns that were so restless that they kept us riding all the time. A few days later he sent us another bunch from Grindstone Creek. Elsie and Jack started sending them in to us right after that until we had 1,500 head. We would get up as soon as we could see and start riding herd. It's a good thing we never had a stampede or our brands would have been scattered all over South Dakota instead of just the southwestern part.

Morphadite Creek was the worst rattlesnake place in the whole country. We would kill as many as twenty a day and sometimes passed them up when we were in a hurry. Sometimes we would carry sticks to kill them with, but most of the time we would hit them with a quirt or the double of a rope and stamp their heads with the boot heel. Bendrickson wore a thick, heavy pair of work boots that were so high and thick a rattler couldn't bother him. When the roundup wagons came in, Welch and Jack were so mad at the snakes that they moved everything over on Frozen Man Creek so we wouldn't have to look around every time we got off our horses.

We held our herd all summer on a range about twenty by thirty miles along Morphadite and Frozen Man creeks where there was the finest grass just heading out. There were lots of wild ducks on the water holes, and we had an old shotgun to pick off a few of them. The young ones were just big enough to fry when we moved in so we lived good on Bendrickson's cooking. Since this range was not claimed by any other ranch, we shoved all other cattle off. After a while Marrington and Williams came along with about 2,000 steers and started to push our herd north. This made Welch awful sore, so he decided to go over to their camp and not just for a friendly drink. He gave them a lot of rough talk and bluffed them out.

The three of us—Bendrickson, Welch, and myself—all worked for Marriot and as hired hands had no right to brand slicks, but I was the owner of a brand and did have that right by range custom. In our herd was a 1,500-pound Red Polled bull and a nice two-year-old heifer that didn't have any kind of a mark on them. Since Welch and Bendrickson wanted in on the deal with me, I offered to sell the bull and split the money three ways if they would put my brand on the heifer. They agreed, but it caused a lot of trouble later.

In August we cut out about twenty carloads of cattle, including eighty steers of mine, and started them for the railroad. There was no bridge between Pierre and Fort Pierre, but the North Western had a big ferry boat called the "Jim Leighton." It took two trips to move all the cattle across the Missouri. Marriot had gone ahead and arranged for a special stock train, which was there when we pulled in. Three hours later we were loaded and the freight was on the way to Chicago. Going on a pass with the stock was Marriot, his ten-year-old son, and myself. At night we stretched out on the long seats running down the sides of the caboose and snoozed pretty good. The next day the train stopped at Baraboo, Wisconsin, where we unloaded the cattle and fed them. United States law would not allow the railroad to keep cattle in a car over thirty-six hours at a time. The lakes sure looked good to us there at Baraboo as we had come from a hot and dry country.

I sold my eighty steers for $2,500 and felt like a rich man. Right away I sent $2,000 to Pa to pay back my loan and went down town in Chicago to buy some clothes and spend a little money. At the Willoughby Hill and Company clothing store I ordered a tailor-made suit of some loud checked goods, some shirts, a new eight-dollar bag, and other trimmings, and started stepping out. I was staying at a cattle-man's hotel on Sixteenth Street, the City Hotel, for one dollar a day. There I ran across the boss of the Pierre Wibaux cattle outfit and did my celebrating with him.

The World's Fair was then being held in Chicago. It was an immense show, and there was a lot to see if one's feet could hold up to do all the walking. People's feet would play out, and they would sit on a bench and take their shoes off and wiggle their toes. I remember some of the exhibits, but mostly to me it was a lot of people walking with their eyes bugged out, trying to get all they could for their money. The Midway shows were very poor. Before one place a barker was making an extra-big talk, and a lot of people were laying down their quarters and going in. I went in along with the crowd. All there was to see was a bed with a man on it asleep. They had people hired to rush in and then they would go out a back exit and come around again. I stood around for a while until some big bully said to me, "Get out of here and tend to your own business." I got out.

We saw some pretty good shows and some bad ones in that ten-day spree. At the auditorium we saw *Ali Baba and the Forty Thieves*, and somewhere else Maude Adams was in *Peter Pan*. At another place we paid fifty cents to see about forty 200-pound colored women, dressed in girdles and rye straw skirts, kick their legs and do the hootchy-kootchy dance. The bald-headed row was a pretty noisy audience. Out at the fair nearly everybody, even the old ladies of the missionary societies, went to see the belly show, "The Streets of Paris."

When a fellow is out in the hot sun eating the dust be-hind a bunch of cows, he can't imagine how he would ever get tired of just pleasure. But after you don't do anything but see girly shows for ten days, you get tired of that, too.

So I headed back to South Dakota pretty well pleased with myself, except that I had to pay my fare back. After riding all night and most of the day, I reached Pierre and went to the old North West Hotel for my first full night's sleep in a good long time.

The next day when I got to Marriot's ranch, Welch and Bendrickson wanted their cut out of the bull that had gone with my cattle to Chicago. I asked them if they had branded the heifer for me as they promised. After they had beat their gums awhile, they finally told me that they had killed the heifer, split the carcass, and used it to drag out a prairie fire. When I told them I would keep the bull money, Bendrickson wanted to lick me. He was an ornery cuss at times. Once at the Morphadite summer camp I had got my dander up and gone after him. He ran out on the prairie and hollered, "Cut out your dogies and go, this fighting has to stop." At another time I cornered him in a cabin and he laid down and covered his head with his hands. He was over six feet and strong as a steer but was about the biggest coward I ever saw. Welch had got mad at him one time, too. After the spring roundup, he asked Bendrickson to wash his two suits of red, all-wool underwear. Bendrickson put them in a kettle with the rest of the dirty clothes and boiled them. When hung out to dry, they shrunk to the size of a ten-year-old boy. Welch was so mad he could have killed him as he had just paid twelve dollars for the underwear. They yelled at each other for about an hour before they finally quieted down. I allow Welch had to sleep raw until after the fall roundup.

As soon as we could get organized, we cut out another trainload of steers and drove them in to Pierre. Welch went along to Chicago this time, and when he got back he would talk for hours about the acts in the girly shows. I suppose it was the hope of going to Chicago at shipping time that kept

89

a good many cowboys eating the dust and fighting blizzards in South Dakota.

AFTER my summer with Marriot in 1893, I was pretty tired of the cattle business. I had put in three years at it and wasn't much more than even with the world. Besides, I had a liking for the girls, but when I went into town with my rough clothes on they wouldn't pay any attention to me. We wore boots made in Olathe, Kansas, Boss of the Road overalls, Stetson hats, and Busby gloves, and usually we were a pretty dirty lot. My idea of a good job was to work in a store so I could go around cleaned up and wear good clothes. Maybe I would have a chance with the girls if I got rid of my cow smells. Owen Wister hadn't yet written his book, *The Virginian*, so we cowhands did not know we were so strong and glamorous as we were after people read that book.

Early that winter I went back to Mount Pleasant, Iowa, and visited with all my relations for a week or two. Pa wanted me to go to school some more as I had only a common school education. That made sense to me so I went up to Burlington and enrolled in the Orchard City Business College. I was pretty rusty in schooling and had never been a very good student. There were about twenty other fellows in school learning bookkeeping, arithmetic, and penmanship, but only three girls. Two of them were sisters that couldn't be separated, so there wasn't much chance for a romance there.

I had a lot of fun for a while that winter when Mrs. Hughes, my landlady, had a visitor from Missouri who was a divorcée and had been on the stage for about ten years. Lela Leake was her name, and she was good company and taught me a lot about the world. I would run errands to the drugstore to get morphine pills for her, and she would tell me not to sample them. When Mrs. Hughes was gone at night, Lela would dress in her tights and dance and sing for me. We went out to dances together, and she taught me to do the polka and other steps. I was sorry when she went back to Missouri.

A German girl named Mary Kuder, who was a servant girl in one of the wealthy German homes, came to visit Mrs. Hughes on her off-day. She invited me over to see her and told me to come to the kitchen door. One night when I was in the kitchen, the girl of the house came out to get some drinks for the guests. She looked at me, made a little face, and said, "Mary, introduce your friend." Mary did, and I said, "Happy to meet you," in my best manner. I met this girl, Flinny Wetzel, out ice-skating a week later. She left her crowd and asked me to skate with her. We talked a lot of nonsense as we skated, and I thought I was getting somewhere in the world when she asked me to come see her that night. She said if she ever caught me in her kitchen again I would be sorry.

I kept going to see her about twice a week, and she seemed to get bossier all the time, telling me how to tie my neckties and comb my hair. One time her father asked me to come see him on Sunday afternoon. He was a well-educated man who had come over from Germany and was interested in the minerals in the Black Hills. I soon found out he knew more about the geology out there than I did. After we had drunk some wine and I was ready to go, he told me I was welcome at his house at any time. I took the old man at his word and spent a lot of time over there. As I walked over to see her I would sing:

> *Gay and stylish girl you see,*
> *Girl of good society,*
> *Not too strict but rather free,*
> *But as right as right can be.*

ONE night when Flinny's folks were gone, she brought out a bottle of her father's wine. She didn't take much of it, but she kept filling my glass. We sat on the sofa and she combed my hair and brushed it. I got a little gay and she got mad and said to me: "Mostly you set and say, yes ma'm, no ma'm, and look like a stuffed owl. Now you drink a whole bottle of Papa's wine and make love like a horse." We had a long squabble and she started me home. I could walk all right, but I was pretty dizzy. Mrs. Hughes helped me get in bed. She was used to that as her old walrus-moustached husband came in that way every night. I never did drink any more of Papa's wine.

It was at the YMCA where I took up boxing that I finally found myself. I would get my ears knocked off for a while, but I learned some of the tricks and got confidence in myself. One day I had a talk with one of the teachers at the business college. He advised me to give up the idea of being a bookkeeper and go back to South Dakota. I went over to ask Mr. Wetzel for advice. He said bookkeeping didn't offer any better prospect than common labor and that the West offered opportunity to a person who stuck with it. Right then I decided to quit school and get back out to the sagebrush country and make good.

On a cold and snowy night in April I pulled into Pierre again. It looked pretty good to me, and it took me a couple of days to get caught up on all that had happened while I was gone. I heard that Sydney Barnes had frozen to death in a blizzard and other news of that sort that was told around town. A few days later I got out to Foster's ranch where I had left my horses and found them all right. I saddled up and rode to Leslie Post Office, or what was once Cheyenne City, looking for a job. At Webb's ranch at the mouth of Ash Creek, old Alex took me on to break ten horses for him. He had been thrown by a bronc and broke both of his arms.

I would tie a gentle one to a bronc so if I got thrown off I wouldn't lose the horse and would have a way of getting home. This was hard work and worth the ten dollars Alex paid me for the week's work.

I went on up Ash Creek to Frank Reed's place. He had just moved in from the Black Hills with a small bunch of cattle and a few range horses. He was new in the business and wanted some help branding and castrating some colts. After working at that a few days, I drifted on over to Midland, a small village of about one hundred people, where I heard that the Madsen ranch wanted a man to help in their roundup starting May 10. They were in trouble. About a dozen of their best saddle horses had disappeared. I started looking along with the rest of the hands and was lucky enough to find the broncs in a little valley fifteen miles southeast. We penned them and never took any chances at losing them so close to roundup time.

On May 8 and 9, we rode to the Bad River at Fort Pierre and got ready to start the next day. Some of the boys went into town that night, lost all their money at blackjack, and got into camp pretty drunk. I still did not have a job to go on the roundup for Madsen, but the boss hired me to wrangle the saddle horses at night until the regular night hawk sobered up. He paid me five dollars for my two nights' work and I went back to Fort Pierre.

Blair and Allison were looking for men to roundup their herd. They were real speculators, had turned 1,500 steers loose the year before and now wanted to hire men to do the dirty work of gathering them for shipment. They had no ranch and only a few horses and they were no good. Several wagons were operating, and Bill Fawsett, a Texan, and I were to pick up the catches and drive them to a central camp on Frozen Man Creek. Blair's son, Bert, and Robert and Cargill Graham, two Nebraska farmers who were almost

93

useless around a bunch of wild cattle, were to hold the cattle there. I couldn't get along with Bert. He thought I rode the horses too hard. He tried to get his father to fire me, but Mr. Blair wouldn't do it. He knew I was doing as much riding as all the rest put together. I got tired of it and quit as soon as we got the main herd together. I heard later that they let about three-fourths of the herd get away, and Blair had to make a deal with other cattlemen to gather them again and deliver them to the stockyards at Fort Pierre.

The country was changing. The depression was on, prices were low, and the range was overstocked. Small cattlemen had an awful problem finding their critters scattered all over the country, and the cold winters made riding after them a hard and disagreeable life. Some of the little ranchers like Charley Foster were going into sheep. They were cheap to buy and easy to keep track of. At least one knew where he was most of the time, and that was more than I knew just then. I still had some cattle in South Dakota somewhere but I wasn't sure just where.

I had turned these things over in my mind and had an idea or two about what I might do. But I still couldn't stand the smell of sheep. Up on Foster Creek I found a good spring and a nice level flat not far from some draws full of ash and cedar trees and decided to file a homestead claim. I dragged logs over to the spring and built a ten-by-eighteen cabin with dirt floor and roof near the soft-water spring. Most of the ranchers used water out of open creek holes that was sometimes alkali and fouled up by stock. This was where the Mississippi Cattle Ranch was later headquartered.

Money was scarce that winter of 1893–94 but I did get a few days' work around at my neighbors. I hoped to get hold of some stock to run on the shares or most any deal to get into the cattle business again. While waiting for spring to come, I decided to replenish my horse supply from some of the strays and slicks I had heard were thick over on Fox Ridge between the Moreau and Cheyenne rivers. That country was unsettled and had nothing in it except a corral or two. My neighbor, Foster, and I thought we might ride up there to see what we could see.

We took a couple of old quilts and some grub on the back of our saddles and made camp on Abear Creek. Foster was hungry for rabbit meat so he took his old pistol down creek and came back with four rabbits stuck inside his shirt. They were full of fleas, and he had a hard time skinning the rabbits and scratching the fleas at the same time. He had to undress, shake his clothes, and jump into the creek to get rid of them. The two rabbits we had for supper were extra good, just like young fried chicken.

The next morning we rode northwest toward where the town of Eagle Butte now is. All along we saw a lot of Abear's and Dupree's branded horses. Farther west we saw an old white mare with bright red ears and her bunch. We didn't try to run them as they were a well-known bunch of outlaws that had been run by a lot of people and had never yet been penned. They roamed over a range about fifty miles by seventy-five miles and were never caught alive. I heard later that someone finally killed the old red-eared mare when he tried to crease her neck bone while she was drinking at a water hole. That's the way most of that creasing turned out. There were a lot of horses in this Fox Ridge country that had been run until they were spoiled. The oftener anyone tried it and failed, the worse they got. Some herds will run until the colts get so hot and tired they die, and some get big puffed-out ankles and are of no use when they are caught. Wild horses are about the wildest animal that lives and are pretty smart, too. Sometimes all you would see of them would be a cloud of dust, as they can see and smell a man as far as he can see with a pair of good glasses.

95

Another bunch of mustangs showed up that had six or eight slicks in it, and they didn't seem so wild. We ran them about five miles until we got in a hilly place, and then the whole herd turned on us. After running them for a few miles, we just gave up on them and watched them high-tail it over the hills out of sight. We had fifteen miles to go to get back to camp, and our horses were so worn out that they couldn't go faster than a walk. It was dark when we got back for a supper of bacon and coffee. Before rolling up for the night, we decided to give up the idea of getting some free horses and to go home. Running wild broncs sure isn't a picnic.

We made the Foster ranch on our tired horses that night for supper. Mrs. Foster made fun of us and told the neighbors about it. For a time we were a good joke. We learned something on the trip, and some years later we tried it and did better. It took our horses about a month to get over it.

Things were pretty quiet that summer for me. I got lonesome with no more to do than looking after five horses and a few cows. Foster had me help him put up hay and dig potatoes. I cut enough cedar posts to fence my 160 acres, fixed up the house some, and did a lot of visiting. That summer I found a big cedar log about thirty inches around, so I decided to make a trough out of it. But it was too heavy for my light team to pull it out of the draw. I worked at it with my ax for three days hollowing it out and then the team pulled it up to the spring. It lasted for years.

The low price of cattle and the lack of work of any kind, along with my lonesomeness, had me pretty low in the fall of 1894. In fact, I got so low that one day I went over to Foster's and told him to keep an eye on my stock while I looked around for a job somewhere. When I pulled out in October, I didn't expect ever to see Foster Creek again. I was going back to the white-collar world.

CHAPTER 7

BACK WITH MY OWN PEOPLE

IN LATE October, 1894, Blair and Allison sent one of the last shipments of cattle out of Fort Pierre that year, and I went along for a free ride to Chicago. There I holed-up for the winter with my sister, whose husband, George, was a real estate broker. He and I would walk over a mile every day to the elevated to go to his office downtown, where he worked hard to get a few commissions.

I hung around the bucket shops buying some wheat now and then on a one-cent margin but didn't come out very well. Sometimes George and I would make as much as fifty dol-

97

lars, and when this happened we would go to the Boston Oyster House and pay fifty to seventy-five cents for a meal. He was quite a city man and would tip the waiters ten or fifteen cents. Since we usually lost money, mostly we went to a saloon at noon and had a five-cent glass of beer and raided the free lunch counter until the waiter hinted that we had killed the nickel we had spent. When wheat went to fifty cents a bushel, we felt sure that it had reached the bottom so scraped up some money and were long 1,000 bushels of May wheat at that price. I sat in a bucket shop one dismal, foggy day and watched the damned stuff sink to forty-eight cents. I knew I was out of the wheat business for good and had exactly $100 to carry me through the rest of the winter. Not long after that I saw one of the big operators, Old Hutch as he was called, peddling apples at a nickel apiece and being pointed out as a man who had been worth millions a few weeks before.

I walked the town looking for a job, but no one seemed to want me. Seeing a sign pointing to an upstairs gymnasium, I decided to go up and get some exercise. The boss and a sickly-looking man were poking at each other with a couple of wooden sticks. I got a chair and watched this feeble performance until the proprietor got through the lesson and came over. He was a university man and an officer in the German army, a fine type of a German. When I told him I wanted work and had been around gymnasiums some, he hired me to sweep out the place every day and to give boxing lessons for beginners.

The cleaning up was easy, but the lessons were tiresome. Most of the students looked like they never had three squares a day. I would take them through the routine with the boss giving instructions from the side of the ring. Once in a while some of the advanced students would sneak a hard lick at me. After the boss told them I would hit them as hard as they

Sioux Indians en route to Fort Bennett for rations, about 1899

hit me, I tried it out on one and got a bloody nose out of it. The boss took over and gave him plenty. I stuck this out for a week and then got my money and quit.

The Chicago people were a bad-mannered lot. They would shove and push each other around in a pretty bad way. These city folks could tell I was a country boy and gave me a rough deal. It seemed that after losing my money in the bucket shop and getting my nose bloodied in the gym, I got a grudge against all Chicago folks. They looked like a bunch of scrub stock to me, so I started pushing and shoving, too, unless the fellow was extra big or looked tough. When I met a person who walked along like he owned the whole street, I met him head on and pushed him out of the way. A few acted hostile and gave me sour looks. Some said, "Look where in the hell you're going." Some just grinned. Pushing these bastards around was good sport, and I guess I was pretty lucky I wasn't arrested or didn't get a good licking out of it. I still think of Chicago as a town of heels and scrubs.

One day I saw an ad in the paper offering twelve dancing lessons for three dollars. Since I was so awkward at dancing that I couldn't join hands and circle to the left and didn't know much more than the divorcée in Burlington had shown me, I signed up. A girl who was a pupil helped me some, and she suggested we try the public dance halls. We went to the South Side to a grand opening of a saloon one night. There was free lunch and beer and a big crowd of working people with a sprinkle of toughs. When the bouncers got busy throwing out the drunks, we got out of there and went to her home. The grand opening was a good show if you like rough stuff.

I was tired of Chicago and homesick for South Dakota, and gave up the idea of a white-collar job. My money was getting so low I went to the Chicago and North Western general office and asked for a pass to Pierre. They asked me

99

what I had done out there. When I told them I had shipped cattle in 1893 and had brought in Blair and Allison's steers in 1894, they gave me a pass. On the way home I stopped over at Burlington and Mount Pleasant and found things bad there. There was no work for anybody, and people were discouraged. Pa was getting a small Civil War pension, and this helped him weather the depression. A lot of people blamed President Cleveland for the hard times, and there was some talk of free coinage of silver as a way out of the mess. I was glad when I got started west again.

It was four o'clock in the morning when I pulled into Pierre. It felt good to be in South Dakota again. The air was good, and with all their faults I liked the Dakota people. The folks in Chicago and Iowa seemed to have bad manners, and the Dakota people didn't have any at all. That is what I liked best about them. I got a ride to Foster's and was soon over to my place. The pack rats were in possession. They had filled the cook stove with dried peaches and beans and put charcoal in my hole in the floor. My horses were still around and everything was all right.

That spring I hired a piece of ground plowed and dropped some corn and potatoes in the edge of the furrow. They came up good. That fall I had about twenty bushels of corn and plenty of spuds, mostly flattened by the tough sod. I fixed my fences, rode around visiting my neighbors, and checked here and there to see who had seen some of my cattle. A lot of company came by that spring, mostly riders looking for work. Some stayed for just a meal, others for a day or two. Most of them were burned out bad with whiskey and disease. The ordinary cowhands worked for six or eight months at thirty to forty dollars a month, then went into town and stayed as long as they could. About half of them would then go to some ranch and get a job doing winter chores. The rest were pimps, living off of some cheap prostitute in Pierre. Texas Siftings was one of them. He lived in a shack down in the red-light district and spent most of his time gambling and drinking in the saloons. Most of them had a dose of clap or pox and some had a double dose. All in all, most of the old-time cowhands were a scrubby bunch. Only the few good ones got into the cow business and made good.

One of my visitors was in a class by himself. He was a graduate of McGill University in Canada and had traveled over a lot of Canada and the Northwest working a few days here and there. I found him a good worker and a fair cook in the two weeks he spent with me. His name was Joseph St. Ange. He was writing a book about his travels, mostly on wrapping paper, and he had a big bundle of it with him. On the title page was written, *Les Voyages de Joseph St. Ange*. He promised me a chapter in his book, but I never got to see it. When he left he thanked me, put his arms around me and put a juicy kiss on both my cheeks, and promised me his friendship forever. Politeness of this kind was rare in South Dakota where we didn't even use the term "mister." I never saw him again.

The university men in the West were rated a rather queer lot. We had heard of Theodore Roosevelt, northwest of us two hundred miles, as a rather locoed fellow who was called the Hoot Owl or Old Four Eyes. Not too far from me lived a Princeton graduate by the name of Wilbur Rudy. He was rather an odd character who had come out there, married a full-blood Sioux, and settled down as a cattleman. Once he shot and killed an Indian in an argument over some hay ground, and his brother, who was a doctor, came out to help in the trial at Pierre. He testified that Rudy had the habit as a boy of hopping trains and had once fallen and hurt his head. The Indians called him Yellow White Man since he had yellow hair and always wore rather yellow clothes.

The jury acquitted him, but his family blamed him for the killing. Three years later he sold his horses to Foster and me and left the country for good.

Most of the white folks had what we called a common school education. Mine was a little scant but was about as good as the mine run. Most of the half-breeds and all of the fullbloods were illiterate. The settlers would rate well in everything but book learning. They had to live in a country from fifty to one hundred miles from town and were pretty much on their own. If anything broke, they had to repair it themselves. If they got into any trouble or had an accident, they had to get out on their own power. It took something to make a living where they had to pay banks 12 per cent interest and a commission on all loans. Anyway, South Dakota was an interesting place and sometimes could be pleasant.

Before the Fourth of July in 1895 some of us met at Harshman and Crockett's horse camp near Lindsay Post Office and took up the matter of a celebration. It would cost us from ten to twenty-five dollars to go to Pierre, so we decided to have one of our own. We put in a dollar or so apiece and on July 3 started the Conklin boy to Pierre in a two-wheeled cart to get a keg of beer and something a little stronger. The next day we sat around waiting for the boy to come. It was a hot day, and we were panting when he got back with his played-out horse about two in the afternoon.

A bunch of the men gathered around the cart and got ready to celebrate. We had to knock in the head of the keg to get our cups filled. The beer was warm and pretty flat. One of the men went over to Lindsay's store and got a big chunk of ice. It still didn't taste right, so we sweetened it with whiskey. We finally got to feeling good and began to holler about being freeborn Americans. One kept shouting, "E Pluribus Unum." Someone asked him what that meant and he didn't know. We had shot off all of our cartridges and were out of anything to do when someone spied a bunch of Texas steers standing in the Cheyenne River. We thought it would be fun to catch some of them and tie cans on their tails, so we rounded up a bunch and had Ed Crocket do the roping. We would get one down, tie several cans to his tail, let him up, and watch him run. Foster had an old horse and a saddle without a horn and was trying all the time to do some roping himself, but he was a little unsteady. Finally, one did run into his loop. He held the rope in his hands and got jerked off his horse. He held on bravely as the steer dragged him through a lot of brush, skinning him up some. Crocket caught the steer and took the rope off. Foster was proud of himself and said if he had a good saddle, he could rope as good as anybody.

One fellow, Hatfield, allowed that he could ride anything with hair on, so we penned a bunch of Harshman and Crocket horses and picked out a wild mare about ten years old. When we had her ready, Hatfield got on; we pulled the blindfold off, and all yelled, "Yippee." The old mare wouldn't buck or do anything, just stood there sullen-like. Someone said, "What she needs is a drink." We threw her down and forced a quart bottle of beer and whiskey down her throat. Hatfield got on again. The old mare kicked at her stomach, hung her head, and finally laid down. We finally gave up and left her alone. Hatfield's claim still stood.

Two Indians came by in a wagon. Some one hollered, "Get across the river where you belong." They were already headed for the ford anyway, but they sure whipped their ponies and got going. We took after them on our horses. When we got close, both were down on their knees laying on the leather. We ran them to the ford, and they kept full speed as they splashed across and were still in a dead run when they went out of sight.

103

One of the men went on down to Lindsay's to get some more ice. When he got back, he told us Lindsay was fit to be tied about canning the steers. He and his wife had been sitting in the shade when one of the critters had come by and chased them in the store. Some of us were mad at Lindsay and allowed we would never trade there again. There was a lot of bad language. I guess we thought we were pretty tough.

Crocket and Harshman wanted all of us to help move the Texas steers out of the Cheyenne bottom so they could save the grass for their horses. They had brought in two hundred or so when they moved in from Montana that spring. We rounded up four or five hundred steers, cut out a few that belonged on the south side of the river, and drove the others over on the reservation side and into the hills. It was late, so we got supper for all who could eat. All some wanted was a little vinegar or soda. We fixed up Foster's scratches with some axle grease, and he was fit as a fiddle even though he looked messy. Everybody went to bed on the floor of the cabin, but a rattler under the floor kept bothering us. When we talked, he rattled. As we had used up all the whiskey which was the only sure remedy for snake bite, we went outside and laid on the ground and let the snake have the house all to himself.

The next morning when I got up, I didn't feel so good. After getting some coffee and a biscuit, I struck out across the prairie for home. Some of the neighbor women talked about the party and said we ought to be ashamed of ourselves. Lindsay was grumpy for a while, but he finally had other things to worry about. We all thought it was a good Fourth of July.

It was time to put up hay, so the next day I started to Fort Pierre in my wagon to get some grub and other things. The boys there had a quiet celebration, they told me. The dance was a pretty sober affair. Young Joe Steiner had come over from Pierre and got so drunk and noisy they threw him in the local ten-by-ten jail. It had walls four inches thick and a small barred window. The marshal just put the drunk in and padlocked the door. The place was filthy, not having any such thing as a water closet or even a bucket. It seemed that this was a good cure for a nuisance drunk but never bothered an ordinary one.

As I drove my wagon back, I kept thinking about our celebration, about my winter in Chicago, and about South Dakota in general. These people might not have manners or money, but they did know how to have a little fun now and then. I was glad I was back with them.

As soon as I got settled down again, I started in haying right away and kept at it for the next month. It was hot and dry, and the grass on the flat was short. I rigged up a grass catcher on the sickle bar of the mower and dumped the hay in wind-rows and bunched it with a rake. By working early and late and Sundays, I hauled in about thirty or forty tons of short-stemmed hay on my basket rack and built pole corrals around the stacks. The squaw corn got to the roasting-ear stage in late July or August, and it was a good change from eating canned stuff after a hard day's work. I also had my share of Juneberries and sand cherries.

Haying over, I went to Pierre to rest up in the shade. There I ran across Hamilton and Coyle from Montana, who had 250 horses out north of town they wanted to sell. I went on horseback to the pasture and bought ten nice two-year-old geldings and a roan work horse for $175. They were Morgan stock and all extra good. That afternoon I saddled one of the broncs and started driving the rest of them across the prairie. That night I penned them at Norvald's on Sans-arc Creek. He liked them and offered me $250 for the bunch, so I sold them right away and made a deal with him to get ten of his best dry cows at shipping time at twenty dollars apiece. I sold these cows right after I got them for $250, so had a profit of $125 for no work at all.

Rudy sent word to me that he wanted to have a try at catching wild horses on Fox Ridge, so I went up to his place on the Cheyenne and we took off from there. We carried some grub on our saddles and led a good horse apiece. On the way we stopped at a dugout Rudy had made on Dupree Creek and the next day went north to Fox Ridge. That country was a fine range land in 1895. There were no settlements, only two pens. Rudy and Rousseau had one apiece on Goose Creek north of the ridge, and later Narcelle had one way west on Red Coat Creek. It was part of the Indian reservation, and a white man was supposed to have a pass before he went on it. Cattle and horses were everywhere, some of them wearing the brands of Dupree, Rousseau, and Narcelle. These men had married Sioux women and had some kind of a right to pasture their stock there.

Rudy knew the bunch we were looking for since he had been there before. About noon we found them and started them toward camp. Our corral was a box washout with a panel of poles at the opening end. We had quite a time getting them in, but finally made it. Two of the mares had Rudy's brand on them, some were slicks, and others had brands that we had never seen before. The next morning we fixed a small pen on one end of the box corral and got Rudy's two mares and their colts in it. Then we roped and hog-tied two big slick colts about two years old and turned the rest of them loose. We knew the big colts would be hard to handle going back, so we gagged them by putting a rope in their mouths and running it over the top of their heads. It was a little cruel, but was one of the ways of handling a wild horse so you could drive him. When we got them to Rudy's, we put his brand on one of the colts and put mine on the other.

By necking him to my saddle horse, I got him home all right.

Some of the neighbors chewed the rag about this as if it was rustling to brand a slick. The actual rule all over the range country was "finders keepers." It took a lot of hard riding to get these wild horses in a pen and get them home so they stayed. Nine times out of ten you earn all you get from hunting wild broncs. I asked some of the old-timers about the range law on this, and they told me it was all right to get colts if they were not sucking their mothers. The fact is that horses were cheap, and a lot of ranchers wouldn't do the hard riding one had to do to keep their colts branded.

The country south of the Cheyenne River was growing. Every year a few more little ranchers moved in and more of them turned to sheep. One of the newcomers in 1895 was a sheepman by the name of Isaac Guyer. He brought his wife and two-year-old daughter and his wife's sister from Brookings, South Dakota, with him and set up near Harshman and Crocket's place. The sister-in-law, Miss Fannie, was the only young woman in the settlement and had been what we called a schoolmarm. She was the kind of a girl who teaches a Sunday school class and sings in the choir. I went over to see Guyer pretty often after I heard he had more than sheep around his camp.

The Guyers thought the cowhands needed some religion, and so they started a Sunday school in their log cabin down the river from Lindsay Post Office. We had what you might call a mixed crowd at the organization meeting. There were a few Indians who couldn't speak English, Mrs. Abear, who was half-French and half-Indian, and a few others. We elected Mrs. Abear president, Kid Rich secretary, and me treasurer. The president was to teach the older ones, and Miss Fannie was to take over the young ones. We spent the rest of the first meeting singing and praying. One Indian made a long prayer, which I couldn't understand, and two

107

others sang a song. Kid Rich and I kept pretty quiet. We took up a collection, and the Kid put it in his pocket.

The next meeting was smaller. The cattlemen didn't like to worship with the sheepmen, and to use a sheepherder's cabin for a church was a little too much. But that wasn't the only problem we had. Mrs. Abear was another. She had been raised a Catholic, but that wasn't her trouble. She couldn't read or write so couldn't teach the grown-up people much. After some praying and singing, we took up another collection, making altogether about seven dollars in the treasury, and Kid took care of it again. The treasurer didn't seem to have much to do.

When it got cold that fall, Miss Fannie went back to Brookings, and the Sunday school had no more meetings. The cattle and horse ranchers said the sheepmen were all sons of bitches anyway and would go to Hell. No more Sunday school and no more Fannie. The Kid took the seven dollars and had Lindsay get him two gallons of whiskey with it. I was at Lindsay when it got there. We sampled it and found it good. He thought we ought to go to the neighbors and pass it around since it was Sunday school money after all. We first went to Conklin's, where we had supper. The jug was left outside and after we ate, the men went outdoors and had a few drinks. The Kid and I went on down the river that night to Hiatt's place. He had a grown-up daughter visiting him from Montana. They insisted that we have supper with them and afterward he had us drink a few out of his jug. He said it was as free as water and for us to drink hearty. It was late by this time but we kept going, and at the next place the Kid hollered and asked if we could get supper. The woman was home alone with the children, but she invited us in for some food. Kid was noisy and rude, but I don't think I was as bad as he was. The woman drove us out, and we went across the Cheyenne to a dugout where a Swede named George Rich lived. We told him we wanted some supper, and he fixed us a good feed, our fourth for the evening. After supper he got pretty full and sang songs for us in Swedish. Kid had learned a lot of songs when he was in the pen at Sioux Falls, and he kept going until poor old George went to sleep.

That night we left old George in a drunken sleep and went to Abear's place, where we fed the stock and went to bed. The next morning, Kid wanted to go over to Dupree's and give them a drink of the Sunday school whiskey. On the way we stopped at Short Log's camp, where he lived with his wives and a few other families. The old man smelled the whiskey and begged for some, but we were afraid to give it to him as we were on the reservation. Finally, the Kid did give him a cupful and swore him to secrecy by having him repeat an oath that Kid had learned in the penitentiary. Of course, Short Log didn't know what all the swearing was about, but it made a nice little ceremony anyway.

Kid pulled a pretty dirty trick on both the Indians and the Abears before we got out of there. He told Short Log that after twenty years of married life without children, Mrs. Abear had finally got pregnant. Abear had a good heart and was so happy he wanted all the Indians to come to a celebration and help eat two fat steers with all the trimmings. Short Log sent a couple of his wives to spread the good news and hollered at the others to wrap his feet in jack rabbit skins and pull on his moccasins. They were going to get in on the free meat right away. After shaking hands all around, Kid and I got out of there and went on up the river.

As we heard the wagons starting across the prairie toward Abear's ranch, I didn't feel so well all over and wanted to get off of the reservation as fast as I could. I told Kid I was sick, besides I had to go home to feed my stock. After a long argument, I agreed to meet him at Dupree's and he took charge of the jug of whiskey and went on his way. It was a relief to get rid of that evidence, as I was afraid of meeting the Indian police. When I got home, I had a long sleep and forgot all about going to Dupree's to celebrate with the Sunday school whiskey.

In a few days I went to the Lindsay Post Office to get my mail and heard that some of the neighbors were pretty sore about us taking the Sunday school money and getting whiskey with it and making a nuisance of ourselves. Some picked me as the goat since they were afraid of the Kid. He found it out and got Irish Tommy to start a rumor that the sheriff was coming out to investigate the butchering of O. P. brand beef. This started a lot of holes being chopped in the ice of Cheyenne River and a lot of good beef packed in these holes. A few were pretty much scared. I got a letter from Fannie after this. She had heard of the whiskey affair and told me all was over between us as she did not want to trust her future to me. I think she shed some tears on the letter. This was probably the best for all as I had no proper place for a lady to live in. I learned a lot from this and tried to keep out of trouble as people never forget your mistakes. When they don't have much else to talk about, they make the most out of a little of nothing.

Several years later, Kid Rich was found dead up on the trail near Cavanaugh's store. No one ever found out who shot him, and I don't think they tried very hard. All of us around there believed he had been brought in by one of the big ranchers to do a killing job or two, and after that was done his boss killed him to keep his mouth shut. Anyway, I couldn't exactly say that when Kid died, religion wasted away around there, but I do know that there was never much talk about Sunday school after this.

CHAPTER 8

A BAD WINTER ON THE PRAIRIE

FROM THE prairie where I lived I could see Fox Ridge forty miles north. Kid Rich had told me there were about 15,-000 horses on that ridge between the Missouri River and the reservation line, and he guessed about 1,000 of them were not branded. It was a great place to get slicks, but unless one owned a pretty good bunch of horses himself, people would raise hell if he went in there and put a brand on any of them. I wanted to go anyway but couldn't get any of the neighbors to go with me. The women folks were still sour on me for that Sunday school money deal and wouldn't let their old men hang around with me much. The only thing to do was to go alone.

I fixed up a pack of bedding, some bacon and canned goods, and a few pots and pans and started out. It was January of '95 but wasn't cold at all. A chinook had taken off the snow and left water in the low places. I went across the river and made my first stop at an Indian camp. They invited me in and gave me some coffee. The old woman had blue eyes and light-colored hair and had a son called Tom Blue Eyes. None of them would tell me where she came from, but she certainly looked like a white woman and might have been picked up by the Indians at one time or another when they were at war with the whites. The old woman told the boy to ask me about Mrs. Abear. I told him that the story about Mrs. Abear going to have a baby was a joke, and when the boy explained it to them, they all laughed. After giving the boy some tobacco and candy, which I suppose the old folks got in on, I pulled out of there.

I made camp at Rudy's dugout that night and rode northwest to the head of Bear Creek. A lot of Hash Knife cattle were scattered among the Dupree and Narcelle stuff, and hundreds of horses were everywhere. A few were wild, but the big bunches were easy to look at. After coming back to Rudy's pens that night, I went to Eagle Butte the next day and took a look from there. I had never seen so many horses and cattle at one time. The whole sight made my mouth water, and I decided to go home and come again with a little help.

Back home I found some one had stayed there overnight and had burned a lot of wood I had cut and had killed a big O. P. brand calf and left me a hind quarter. They had been in a wagon, and I think they were killing prairie chickens for the market. The beef tasted pretty good, as I had been living on bacon for quite a while.

112

In February I got a letter from J. M. Collins, a station agent at Ossian, Iowa. He wanted me to run some steers on shares and sent a contract for me to sign. This looked like a good deal to me, so I signed it and sent it right back. In March, 217 cattle loaded in five boxcars got into Fort Pierre and I was there to meet them. Collins had sent his brother Ed and a cousin Tommy along with them. We got some help and put the Link and Pin brand on them before we set out home. Ed and I started out, and I gave Tommy a ten-dollar bill to get some grub for us. We found out when we went to eat that night that you can never trust an Irishman with other people's money. He had got a two-gallon jug of whiskey, a ten-cent box of crackers, and a little meat. We made out all right for supper, but after that we got hungry for bread. Whiskey is good, but it doesn't stick to the ribs.

We camped the first night on the north branch of Willow Creek about eighteen miles from Fort Pierre. It was windy and chilly and the coyotes came up close to do their howling. Tommy was scared, but Ed said he wasn't at all. There were no settlements between Pierre and my place, and to these Iowa boys it did seem awful lonely. The second night we camped at the Sansarc forks, and Tommy tried to keep his spirits up with whiskey. He was homesick and said over and over, "There ain't nothing here but sky and prairie, nothing but prairie and sky," and wanted to go back home. The next day we were so hungry we left the cattle to themselves and rode on in to my place and cooked up a lot of grub. Ed and I backtracked and moved the cattle to the north prong of Sansarc Creek and left them there for the time. Tommy was still worried about the prairie and sky, but Ed seemed all right. They stayed a week with me before going back. I told Tommy he could cure his baldness if he would drink sagebrush tea. He gathered two big sacks and took them along with him, but in Pierre someone told him it was no good, and he threw the sacks away. By the time they were getting on the train both of them said they had sure had a big time. But Tommy still thought there was too much prairie and sky out in that country.

That spring the roundups started May 10 as usual, and I joined some of them. I followed the H. O. Holcombe wagons for ten days on Mitchell Creek and then went back with George Holly and found a dozen of my Link and Pin steers. George Jackson wanted some help with his little roundup, so I went over a few days, did some branding, and found a few of my critters. The cattle looked good that spring. The grass was better than usual, as so many of the ranchers were shoving their stuff across the Cheyenne on to the reservation even if it was against the rules.

After a summer of putting up hay and riding grubline, I went out with the fall roundups the same way. The last part of October I went with a crew working the Paradise River north of the Cheyenne to get the cattle they had moved on to the reservation. It was cold and there was about a half-foot of snow. It was impossible to keep warm even with winter clothes and a lot of whiskey. When the night wrangler let all the saddle horses get away, the roundup broke up and everybody was pretty sore about the whole deal.

We had an election at Lindsay on November 4. We had twenty voters and most of them got drunk that day, knocked over the table, and nearly had a good fight over who was better, Bryan or McKinley. I was a clerk, so let the stuff alone and didn't argue with anyone. We clerks stuck to crackers and sardines, and I read some of the papers that were in the post office.

The fall of 1896 was cold and stormy. It snowed and drifted and snowed some more. People were scared that there wouldn't be any stock left alive by spring. Some of them

Siberts (left) and Ray Chisholm roping a bronc

started roundups in November and shipped out all they could find. There was a fair market for feeder steers, a three-year-old being worth about thirty to thirty-five dollars, so some of them didn't come out so bad at that.

Guyer and Harshman had about 1,500 sheep east of Lindsay and wanted some help while they went to Pierre after supplies. I battled my way through the drifts about the middle of November and found Mrs. Guyer and a twelve-year-old boy from the orphan's home, Ray Chisholm, glad to have some company. Another big snow fell the next day, and the drifts were five to ten feet high all around. I hauled hay about ten miles with a poor team to the stinking sheep and cussed myself for ever taking such a job. After shoveling snow and breaking tracks, I would get in at night with a played-out team and 800 pounds of hay. Ray would herd the sheep and try to keep them in a sheltered place. He froze his face, ears, and hands pretty bad, and I felt sorry for the little fellow. Guyer and Harshman stayed on in town and told someone they were resting up awhile and that they had a good man with their sheep.

On Thanksgiving day I got up early and saw that another blizzard was moving in on us. It was so fierce that you couldn't face it head on. I told Mrs. Guyer we shouldn't take the sheep out that day as we couldn't get them to face the blizzard coming back in that night. The cabin was in a bottom sheltered by a lot of brush and cottonwood trees, and I thought we should put the sheep there. She said the sheep must go up the draw where they had always been taken. We had quite a row, but she had her way and sent Ray out with them. He took them about a half mile and into a side draw and stayed with them until noon, when I went up there so he could come to the house to eat. His face was nearly a solid scab from frostbites. The storm got worse as I started early that afternoon to pen the sheep. We tried to drive them but

115

they wouldn't face the wind and snow. Before dark, I gave up, went to the house, and told Mrs. Guyer she could pen the sheep if she wanted them in. She took a broom and sailed out of the house, and I stayed in where it was warm. About dark she and Ray came in, but the sheep were still up in the draw.

That night I slept with Ray while Mrs. Guyer worried about the sheep. He told me he hoped all the sheep died so he wouldn't have to herd them. The next morning we found about one hundred in fair shape and by digging around where we saw a hole in the snow found another hundred. When we dug them out they seemed lively at first, but most of them died. Their wool was wet and it froze. After working all day, we got the sorry outfit into the pen. I decided I wasn't needed there any more, so went to my place to see how things were and came back to the sheep camp the next day. Harshman and Guyer were back and wanted to jaw me about the deal. Mrs. Guyer was bawling. I told them to pay me, and after some pretty loud words I got my one dollar a day. This wound up my sheepherding and my dealings with the Guyers. Ray Chisholm ran away in the spring, and so the Guyers had to stew in their own juice after that.

The winter of 1895–96 was a hard one. In January, instead of getting a chinook wind that took away most of the snow, we got more blizzards and cold weather. Ranchers started feeding some of their hay, but no one had enough to last long. Cattle hung around where the haystacks had been and bawled night and day. Some laid down in the snow and got their legs wet, which then froze and made them lame. Horses pawed through the snow and got feed, so they stood the winter well. The cows would follow the horses around and try to get any grass left and would eat the horse manure. But the losses were awful high everywhere. La Plante, who had trailed 2,300 steers up from Texas, lost all but 100 or so, and like a lot of other ranchers, he never quite got back up again. All the people who loaned money on cattle were hopeful. They had been told that stock could winter in South Dakota with a loss of no more than 10 per cent.

The fifty steers of mine that hung around my place were in good condition because they had some reserve fat on them when they started the winter. When I went over to Rudy's to check with him, he told me that he had heard that all cattle north of the river were doing better as the snow wasn't so deep there. He told me I could use his dugout if I wanted to ride that way, that there was flour, sugar, and meat there to use. I dressed up warm in a sheep-lined overcoat, fur mittens, and overshoes, and took two tanned cowhides for my bed, and riding one horse and leading another started out.

I got to the dugout that night late. It was good and warm since Rudy had replastered it with mud that summer. I lit a candle and built a good wood fire and was warm in no time. I thawed out some canned milk, potatoes, and canned fruit, made some coffee, and settled down for the evening. The only bad thing about trips like this was what would happen to me if I got hurt or crippled so I couldn't get on my horse. The next morning I rode north and saw that the stock was faring better there than below the river. There was less snow and more grass, and they could shelter in the brush and canyons. Every now and then I saw where a wolf had killed a colt or cow and had a feast. On Virgin Creek I ran across some Indians hunting. They had killed a young antelope and invited me to eat with them. Raw liver with the squeezings of the gall bladder on it was extra good they thought. It didn't look so good to me that way, so I roasted a piece over the fire and liked it. These hunters were in good humor since they had got a lot of meat to eat and jack rabbit skins to make moccasins out of. They gave me the hind leg of an antelope and offered to put me up for the night in their tepee. Since it looked colder than my dugout, I decided to go back there. When I left, they were doing pretty well with the Bull Durham I gave them.

Going home the next day, I rode with my eyes nearly shut to keep from going blind. The big Arctic owls would follow me for miles, and when I would shoot a jack rabbit or a prairie chicken, they would gather around right away. Twelve days after leaving home, I was back again. I felt pretty good about the cattle for I had about 125 north of the river and I was sure they would come through the winter.

It was lonesome in my cabin, and there was nothing to do. I read all my books and papers over again, smoked a lot of tobacco, and trapped two or three coyotes a day. Before winter was over, I had $150 worth of furs and traded them to Lindsay for grub and clothes. A few skinners were out working on the frozen cattle, but the owners didn't like that very much. They didn't trust a skinner to operate only on the winter kill. Skinning a frozen cow looked like a poor way to make a living to me, so I stayed away from it and went to Pierre for a while.

The ranchers in town were not worried much about the winter losses, not having been far from the saloons and backrooms all winter. They sat there and played cards and drank cheap liquor day after day without much change. A show company was in town and put on shows for a week while I was there. Susan B. Anthony came and talked on woman's rights. She was one of the ablest speakers I ever heard. But a week of this was enough for me, and I went back to my trapping and reading until spring came again. It was the worst winter I ever went through.

WHEN the ice goes out of the Cheyenne River, it is quite a show. For ten miles one can hear the cracking and booming as the big ice cakes, thirty inches thick and fifty feet across, are thrown up by the spring thaw and pushed out over the bottom land. This is the sign of spring, and everybody begins to get squared around for the May roundup. I got my six horses in the pasture and bought three more from Chauncy Bacon for twenty dollars apiece. He had got them as wages for breaking horses all winter over at Hot Springs. Now I was ready to follow the wagons and, with a lot of others, to see what the bad winter had done to us.

I first went to Fort Pierre to join the small ranchers' pool outfit on Bad River. There were reps from every ranch, big and little, in the Northwest, and Tex Hamphill was the boss. When I got there the corrals were full of horses, and a lot of the men were in town having a last fling. There was a lot of gambling and rowdying, and if one could stand the drunks, one could have a good laugh or two just looking on.

One of the cowpunchers, Mexican Joe, had a new bedroll all tied up in nice shape lying on the front porch of one of the stores. Dutch Van Metre and a few of the boys were having a look at it while Joe was in playing cards. They got an idea all at once when they saw a cow coming down the street with a bell on. Dutch and his pals caught her, backed her up to the porch, tied the bedroll to her tail, and turned her loose. The critter went bawling and kicking up the street. When the drinkers and gamblers in the saloons heard all the yelling, they poured out into the street to enjoy the fun. All but Mexican Joe. He was mad and wanted someone to tell him who did it. Dutch pointed to Buck White, the only colored man in town. Joe jumped on him, but he was stopped before much damage was done. Several of the boys got on their horses and brought the cow back up the street. The bedroll was pretty muddy, but Joe was glad to get it back anyway. Several of the crowd bought drinks for him and Buck, and then Joe went back to his faro game. He wouldn't go back to the cow camp until he was broke.

Seeing things were getting a little dull, Tolly Maupin set out to pep up Main Street by riding his horse up and down the only piece of board sidewalk in town. The marshal dusted off his star and led the horse out into the street. Tolly started to swing a short strap with a buckle on it, and when it got whirling good, he hit the marshal in the face with it. The marshal swore and cussed, pulled Tolly off of the horse, got him down and rubbed dirt in his eyes. This started a free-for-all. Burgess looked out from his drugstore and came out in a hurry. As he came out the door his wife got hold of his coattail and hung on. She slid along to the edge of the porch and let go, and Burgess plunged right into the middle of the fight and was promptly knocked down. He got up and ran back to his store quicker than he came out, his wife putting in a few remarks suitable to the occasion. Burgess had a bloody nose, and Tolly had a black eye. In an hour the whole thing was forgotten. People wondered what next.

Fred Fruh got to town with a half-wild team of broncs hitched to a buckboard. He didn't tie them good, so they got loose and started running down the street. They were about to run into a surrey with some ladies in it when Dave Yokum made a quick move and fanned them away with his hat. This was a close call for the women. Someone caught the team and put them in a corral. Old Fred didn't know anything about it. He was busy smoking his pipe and drinking a few glasses of beer.

Horses were an important part of the roundup. Every outfit had quite a string of extra saddle stock. They weighed from 900 to 1,100 pounds and could make sixty miles in a half-day's work and as much as ninety to one hundred in one day if pushed. Most of the range stock was on the small order, but Morgan and Thoroughbred blood was showing up in the horse herds. There were a few good ponies, mostly paints that had come from the Indians. We had a handful of

Appaloosa with the spotted rumps that had come in there
from the mountain country farther west. Droves of range
broncs came into Pierre at roundup time, and while they
went through the block and a half of business part of town,
the loafers got off the porches and the sidewalks and let
them pass.

We finally got out of town with the wagon and moved
to Willow Creek, where we worked a few cattle that people
were close herding and got out all that they did not want to
hold. The drunks came struggling out, one or two at a time,
and were pretty unsteady for a day or two. The next day
I rode the long circle north to Bad River while the wagon
moved to Lance Creek Holes. Already we had a good sized
herd of six to eight hundred, mostly Texas dogies and cows.
In the afternoon we branded calves. Sometimes we worked
our day herd so the different reps could send their brands to
the home range. I had a good string of horses for the first
time this year and found it easier as I could go out on the
circles on a gallop and ride the fifteen or twenty miles that
way. Most everybody was in good humor except Ed Delehan. He had a mean streak and tried to pick on several of us.
He carried a gun and seemed to have it in for Jim Hayes, a
good-natured Cherokee who was easy to get along with.
This went on for several days until Jim got his gun out and
called Ed down. It looked like there would be a shooting,
but Ed backed down, took his gun off, and put it in his bedroll. This was a pretty big comedown for a bully. Jim just
laughed at him and told him he just was not of fighting stock.
Next day Ed cut his cattle out of the day herd, got his horses
and bedroll, and started back to his ranch. He didn't come
back, but his outfit sent another man to represent it in the
roundup. This suited everybody as most of the folks didn't
want trouble, but they didn't want to be bullied, either.

Delehan worked in the range country for several years

after this affair. Once he and another cowpoke called Cimmaron started to shoot up Fort Pierre. They were drunk and were standing in front of Hayes Saloon. Lou Bentley, the marshal, got a shotgun and took a shot at them. Just at that time Nick Fahls walked out of the saloon to see what was going on and was hit with a big load of buckshot and killed. Delehan was arrested and put in jail. He wanted me to go on his bond, but I refused. I am sure he always hated me, but we never had any trouble. Later, he was turned loose. He afterward married and moved to the island. Blood poison finally killed him. This relieved me as it might have saved me the dirty job.

The roundup worked west. The Norvalds and I sent out cattle north to Sansarc Creek from our Frozen Creek camp. It was hard work riding the long circle every day, standing guard two hours every night, and up at daybreak to get on a bronc that had to unlimber before he could get going for the day. The cattle owners were getting gloomier all the time as they saw that about half of their stock was all that lived through the winter. A lot of them realized for the first time that they were broke.

At Grindstone Creek I left the roundup and took steers belonging to me and some Fort Bennett ranchers toward home. It took me three days to get to Sansarc Creek, where I left them and went on home to get some rest. A roundup is hard work and long hours. It always seemed to me that I had to work on the dusty side of the herds and my turn at calf wrestling was a mean one.

A lot of this Dakota work was tough but interesting. Mostly there was plenty to eat, but the water was pretty bad. We usually had good tarp, tepee tents to sleep in, and slickers to wear, but we often got wet and had to sleep that way at night. In the storms, lightning always seemed to hit close to us. Once in a roundup near Fort Pierre, Dick Wickert was hit and killed. The body was taken to town and laid on a counter in an old store building. We would walk up and look in the window to see it. There were no undertakers in these western towns so burials had to be hurried up. Another time a boy named Eddie was on the way to my place and at Frozen Man Creek was struck by lightning and killed. A lot of range stock was hit every year.

In the hopes of finding more of our cattle, a bunch of us next went to the northwestern part of South Dakota to take part in the roundups there. This was the range where the big outfits operated. Twelve of us took about one hundred saddle horses and bedrolls and went up through the reservation to Narcisse Narcelle's ranch, where we stayed two nights. We heard the wagons were working about seventy-five miles farther on, but no one knew where, so we went on up through an unsettled country. The first night we came to the OHO camp of the Holcombe Brothers of Rapid City, where we found two hands in charge. They fed us good, which was quite a job as we had not had any dinner. They didn't know where the big outfits were exactly but allowed they were about seventy-five miles on northwest.

A dim trail led northwest from there, so we followed it most of next day. None of us had ever been in that country before so had quite a sight looking at it. There were no ranchers' cabins in the whole country and it was everybody's pasture. We saw brands from the states of Montana, Wyoming, the Dakotas, and Canada. About four in the afternoon we found the outfit we were looking for. There were eight different wagons strung along a small creek, and each wagon had a day herd of 2,000 to 4,000 and from 300 to 500 saddle horses. They had been working this country all spring and had met here to get each outfit's cattle bunched to send to their home range. The whole bunch worked together for a few days going east, and we went along. You can cover a lot

123

of ground with about two hundred men making the circles. My bunch worked with the OHO outfit as it was the one nearest our country.

One man from England was there to see about some loans that had been made by his bank. He had a good string of horses furnished by some big outfit. Sometimes he would work along good and then all at once would take off after a jack rabbit or a wolf. Several times he got lost, and his keepers would have to look him up. Once he was lost all night. It got to be a joke. Someone would ride up to a wagon on a high run and holler, "Have you seen Lord Limber-prick?" and someone would say, "He went that way." I think his outfit lost a lot of money as these wagons had kept a tally all over the country and knew a lot of cattle were gone for good. The winter of '96 made a lot of little ones out of big ones in the whole Northwest.

We worked on east and would split each morning into eight wagons, as we called a roundup crew. Each outfit would gather a bunch and then take their cut out of it and move it to their own wagon. In the afternoon, each crew branded its calves and put its own stuff in the day herd. A lot of cattle were turned loose on the same range where they were found, and left there. It was a whole day's work to rework these day bunches and get all the cattle in the right herds. We hadn't found any of our brands yet.

It rained every day and night for the next ten days. The creeks were so full of water that we couldn't move. One night when we were camped near a small rancher's wire fence, lightning hit close by. We were in bed at the time and heard the horses running, posts cracking, and some squealing. In the morning the night hawk brought in about half of the horses—the rest were gone. About forty were cut so bad they had to be shot while about that many were turned loose to live or die. Over four hundred horses had hit the wire fence on the run, and it ruined a lot of good horse flesh. It was the bloodiest sight any of us had ever seen. The cattle roundup stopped, and a horse roundup started. All day we looked for the lost animals. I found my two about fifteen miles north, but a good many were lost completely. We moved away from that wire fence as fast as we could.

For days the horses were spooky, and it took extra night wranglers to hold them. As it rained all the time, there wasn't much we could do anyway but herd horses. After it cleared up, we had quite a time drying out the bedding and cleaning off the mud.

We moved on through an open country full of cattle, horses, deer, antelope, coyotes, and big gray wolves. Some of the prairie dog towns were five or six miles across. When we were on circle, the wild horses would start running as soon as they saw us, and a few of the outlaw bands just left the country. A few old outlaw Longhorns got in the day's catch now and then, and when they wanted to leave, they just left. Once when we had four in the bunch and they started walking out, an old Texas roper caught one of them by the front foot and turned him over. A horn was broke off and hung only by a piece of skin, but the critter got up and started off anyway. I was holding the cut and tried to turn them back, but they wouldn't turn. The old steer with the broken horn took in after me and chased me about a mile. I made good time until he finally gave up.

These Longhorns were all colors, but the brindle blue ones were really wild animals. Fred Dupree still used the blue bulls for breeding. We found one bunch of about forty with a big blue bull in front standing guard. I rode too close, and he charged and ran me about a mile. By keeping only the best and most rugged for breeding, old Fred's Texas stock was extra good and his four- and five-year-olds sold near the top on the Chicago market. In the fall roundup the men would try to get the outlaws in the beef herd. The good ropers would throw them and knock their horns off and sometimes sew their eyes shut or cripple them so they could not run.

Dupree had a big brown bronc that bucked some and he wanted me to ride him. At first I worked easy with him around the camp. When we rode on a stiff lope up to a high butte where we started the circle from, he seemed all right. No sooner had we started from there than he started to buck. He went high and sunfished, but I managed to stay on minus a hat. Someone brought me the hat, and after that I had no more trouble. I rode him every other day after that with no more monkey business than a little jumping around when I got on.

When these outfits had worked across the reservation to Dupree's range, we had it easy. Most of his stock was bunched not far from Fox Ridge, and the calves were already branded. The cattle belonging west of the reservation were started back, and my gang belonging south of the Cheyenne took our herd with us. I left my bunch of forty along the river and went on home to rest up.

After the spring roundup, the only people who could hold their heads up were the horse ranchers. Half of all the range cattle were dead, and the rest of them were so thin you could count the ribs. Most everybody, and that included the bankers who had mortgages on about every herd, thought it was because the stock was mostly from Texas and not used to Dakota winters. Give them a few years and all would be well. I didn't look at it that way. When I saw Foster, Lindsay, and others drive big herds of horses south from the Indian reservation and saw the way they had wintered, I decided a bronc was a better bet than a cow in South Dakota.

CHAPTER 9

GETTING INTO THE HORSE BUSINESS

A FTER the roundup of 1898, things were pretty quiet all summer. I had another acre of prairie broke and planted more squaw corn and potatoes in the furrows. Putting up the hay was as hard and as hot as usual. Living there on the flat was a lonesome life, and more than once I thought my neighbors who had a wife to keep house for them were pretty lucky.

The Norvalds had a place at the forks of Sansarc Creek and another on Dupree's bottom north of the Cheyenne River. They would go back and forth by my place and would stop to visit, eat, and get some of my good spring water. They had two girls, Stella and Ida, who were a little shy of me after hearing some of the tales the gossips told about me and Kid Rich. One night after dark I heard some talking and hollering. I went out and found the girls and their brother, Yon. They had started from the Dupree bottom over to the Sansarc place with an old pony and a buggy. On a steep hill the pony had balked, and they had worked for several hours to get it to move. Finally they unhitched him, left the buggy at the bottom, and led him up to my place. They were tired and thirsty and not so sure they should come to a cabin where a bad egg lived. I got supper for them, bedded the girls down in my pile of blankets, and Yon and I slept outside. The next morning I pulled the buggy up the hill with one of my horses, and the old pony took them on home.

Late that summer I did a little writing back and forth with Collins, the man who had sent the steers out to me on the shares. He wanted to move the critters to Iowa and feed them that winter. It looked like a money-maker to me, so I told him to count me in. He rented a big feed yard ten miles south of Sioux Rapids with water tanks and corncribs. While I was rounding up all the cattle I could find and loading them at Pierre, he filled the cribs with fifteen-cent corn and two-dollar hay. On the way I bought six big bulls for fifteen dollars apiece and two hundred shoats to follow the steers.

After I got squared around in Sioux Rapids I got acquainted with the Swedes, Norwegians, and Germans around there. There were a lot of nice girls and some pretty tough boys. Between going to Storm Lake after linseed meal and feeding the cattle, I got in my share of barn dances and literary society meetings. When I was in town once, Ole Larson hollered out to me to come into his house and have a drink before I went out to the feed lot. He pulled out a jug of alcohol and poured the mugs half full. Then he filled them the rest of the way with water, put in some sugar, and stirred. As he licked the spoon he said, "This will fix you up." It sure did. It was like swallowing a kerosene lantern. Going home, I started the team out on a trot up the hill and put them in a lope the rest of the way. When I got to my boarding place in the country, I hollered to the Sutton boys to come out and help me. They said I was full and put the team away for me. Alcohol was used for a good many celebrations at that time since it sold for about one dollar a gallon while whiskey sold for that much a quart. These people seemed to live long and happy anyway.

In April we dehorned the cattle and shipped everything to Chicago. The Spanish-American War helped the prices some. After paying my bills and squaring up with Collins, I had a little money left and felt prosperous enough to take my first Pullman on the way back. It cost two dollars and was worth it.

When I got back to Pierre that spring, I bought a thirty-dollar horse and rode out to my cabin. The pack rats had been busy, and the grub was pretty low, after visitors had come and gone all winter. Three of my horses were gone, but I found about twenty left-over cattle on Sansarc Creek. I didn't join the roundups that spring as I had worn down my four horses looking for the other three. When one of the roundup crews made a mistake and put Billy Borst's brand on a big, bull calf of mine and left me a little runty one, I made up my mind again to get out of the cattle business. They called it an honest mistake.

One day I rode over to Foster's sheep camp. He was in bad. A pen full of sheep had piled up, and about twenty of them had died. There he was skinning them, and they were getting pretty stale. I took a look at the smelly mess and said,

"Go to it, that's the way I got my start." He was already pretty disgusted with things, and this made him madder. He came right back and said, "No, you didn't, you got your start stealing horses." There wasn't much more to say, so I left the corral and went to the house. His wife had washed the dinner dishes, but she cooked a meal for me. I told her what we had said to each other, and she allowed it would smell better around there if she had married a horse thief instead of a sheepman, and if they stayed with sheep much longer they would be completely broke. Not long after that, they sold out and moved to a farm in Michigan. Even though they had a ten-room house, they missed the prairies, and finally moved to New Mexico where they could hear the coyotes howl.

The sheepmen were bringing in more sheep and new ranchers were coming in every spring. Most of the new ones had their families with them, and they lived in the little log houses with sod roofs the way the rest of us lived. Those who could moved their families into Pierre for the winter so the kids could go to school. The rest of them just let the kids grow up without any schooling. It was a lonely life, and a lot of them couldn't take it. One man left for Pierre one winter day to get grub and left his wife and three children in the fourteen-by-fourteen dugout. When he got back he found the sod roof had collapsed, and the whole family was dead underneath. He dug the frozen bodies out and hauled them to Pierre for burial. It was a horrible thing to have happen—even to a sheepman.

Old man Kinneki, who had some sheep over on Frozen Man Creek, made a habit of hiring floating herders. He would work them for six months or a year and to save paying wages would then kill them. It was said around that he got rid of eight or ten that way and made himself a lot of money. This went on until one of the floaters was missed by his friends.

The XO Ranch in 1900

Siberts' horse herd in 1900

Officers came out to search for the body. Kinneki got scared, dug up the corpse to move it to a safer place, and was tracked down. He was sent to the pen for life, but after being made a trusty, walked off and was never heard of again.

Among the cattlemen the sheepmen were outcasts. They had a suspicion that the sheepmen didn't eat much mutton but did eat a lot of beef. Poison was put out for the sheep, and there was a lot of bad feeling on both sides. I kept on friendly terms with both sides, and at one time or another helped Foster herd his flock when one of his men walked out on him. But I always hated the silly things. One day when I went over to the Foster's I saw three little white things running around the house. When I got near, I found out they were two naked children and a pet lamb. They were all drinking out of the trough and ran for the house, all three going, "Baa, baa, baa." I hollered, "Baa, baa." The Missus came out of the door and scolded the kids for taking off their clothes. I stopped awhile and visited, but we used English for that talking.

That fall while I was in Pierre helping solicit cattle for the Chicago commission firm of J. C. Church, I had the chance I had been wanting for a long time. A man and a boy were driving a bunch of mares through town, and I helped them along. It was a good bunch. There were several Morgan mares and a gray Percheron stallion besides a good work team and two saddle horses. I bought the thirty-seven head, with twenty gray colts thrown in, for $565. The bank did not make a practice of loaning money on horses, but I talked them out of $200 so I could close the deal.

On my way home with my little herd I met another of one hundred horses going east. It was owned by Mrs. Killian, and she was along riding in a spring wagon. Her two daughters, dressed in boys' clothing, were doing the herding. They were good lookers. One of them told me she hadn't had much schooling and wanted to get to town so she could get an education and wear dresses like the other girls. Mrs. Killian said there was no market at all for horses in Wyoming and she was going east to sell at her first chance. She wanted ten dollars a head and would throw the colts in. I would have bought them, but $1,000 is a lot of money to a fellow who has just strained his credit to borrow $200.

Near the Rood ranch I saw another herd of horses. This bunch had five or six hundred in it and was owned by an English outfit from Inyon Kara Creek in Wyoming. The riders looked at mine and called them good but thought a man was a damn fool to start in the horse business when there were millions for sale everywhere at your own price.

I was pretty busy that fall taking care of the horses. For a while I herded them every day and penned them every night. As there was plenty of grass and water, they weren't hard to hold. One day when I went to the Lindsay Post Office, one of the little boys came out and said, "Bruce, you are going broke. You're crazy to buy horses. Papa said so." This was the opinion of about everybody. But I was tired of chasing cows all over South Dakota and finding half of them dead in the spring. And I sure didn't want to smell sheep all day long, year in, year out, the way some people had to do to make their living. Besides, I knew how well Ben Ash had done with horses, and I thought a lot of him. He had paid twenty dollars a head for about 2,000 a few years back, had kept them three or four years, and sold them at forty dollars apiece, besides the increase. It looked to me that if I stayed with horses a few years, I might be worth something.

In November we had a bad blizzard. The next day my horses were gone. I trailed them in the snow for twenty miles southeast and then lost the tracks. For a week I hunted everywhere for them, but found no trace. I knew where they had come from so decided they had gone back to their foaling range. I went up Cheyenne River to Leslie, on to Rood's ranch, and over to Deadman's Creek to Mark Spencer's old place, and there I found them. It seemed the best thing to me to leave them there to save a lot of riding all winter. I cut out my saddle horses and work team and brought them home. In the spring I expected to move the mares down to my range so they could have their colts there. Then my trouble of chasing them would be over.

When I got word that Tom Tolton at old Fort Bennett wanted to sell his horses, I went to his place to look them over. He had a good bunch of mixed stock and offered them to me at eleven dollars apiece, colts thrown in. I bought thirty-five head having various brands on them and was to pick them up the following April. That winter I cut ash poles in the canyons and fixed up the corrals, hired Rudy Meyers to work for me starting April 1, and got ready for the spring.

In April I moved the Tolton horses home and then went to Deadman's Creek for the others. They had wintered well and were about ready to have colts. About this time Jeff Carr came along and made me a good offer for my place and I sold it to him. Then I bought another one about six miles south on Sansarc Creek. It had a small dugout on it that wasn't more than five and one-half feet high. We were always bumping our heads on the roof. This can be right aggravating. One day I hired a carpenter to build me a house I could stand up in. He did a fair job and made a log house twenty by twenty with a board floor and a dirt roof. There was even tar paper between the layers of sod, and this helped keep the rain from coming through. It was the best house I had ever had in South Dakota. After getting the corrals fixed up, we got along good.

One of the mares kept trying to get back to Fort Bennett to have her colt. We watched her close, but one day when

133

we were eating dinner, she started out on a trot with about twenty others following her. I galloped after them but couldn't get them turned until I got to Minnecazhe Creek fifteen miles away. When I got them home, we penned her. She nickered a lot that night, but the next morning she had a wobbly-legged colt. After that she never caused any trouble.

After foaling time I counted 150 mares and colts in my herd. That included the Indian pony mares which I had picked up from time to time. When bred to a good stallion, they produced extra-good colts. It was that crossbreed that made up most of the saddle stock of South Dakota.

I plunged further into the horse business in the summer of 1899. Jeff Carr of the Mississippi Ranch had me ride for him a few times and paid me twenty-five dollars a time. Then I borrowed $500 from Rudy. With this money I kept buying horses every time I saw some for sale. A bad job of castration cost me four of them, as I had been careless and used a dirty knife. This taught me to keep my knife clean and to use some carbolic acid in water for disinfectant after that.

There was hardly ever a time but what a horse or two was gone. They would stray away and get mixed up with others. Later I would hear of one being on some other range. This called for a lot of riding and inquiring all over the country. In August, when it got hot and dry, we had to drive my herd north of the Cheyenne. The Sansarc was low and boggy and so full of alkali that it wasn't fit for man or beast to drink. We started them north slow-like, but as they got near the river they began to trot and finally to gallop. They pawed the water and drank for a long time. After that, it was no problem keeping them around there.

AFTER a summer herding horses in South Dakota a man can get about as much prairie and sky as he can stand. When that time comes, he has to go to town and blow off some steam, sit in the shade, and talk to some other human beings. I was in that shape in August, 1899, and started out early one morning to do something about it.

I rode into the hot wind all morning and at noon stopped on Bad River to eat my lunch. The river was low and most of the holes were dry. Seeing some cattle standing in one, I shooed them away, got down on my belly, and filled up with that warm, dirty water. The horse had more sense than I did, for he pulled his muzzle out right soon. The water made me sick, and I vomited all of it up. I pulled off my clothes and soaked in the water hole for an hour, then I felt better but not well enough to eat my lunch.

Two or three miles down the river was George Mathieson's ranch. I rode in there, and Mrs. Mathieson gave me some ice water. I'll bet I drank a gallon of it before I was filled up. They invited me for supper and the night. It was so hot that all the men slept outdoors. Bawley Mathieson slept with the colored hand, Buck White. They kidded him about it, but he said Buck had the best bed and he liked him and they all could go to hell.

The weather of South Dakota at its worst is described as hotter than hell in the summer and colder than hell in the winter, and sometimes in the spring the wind blows like hell. When the grass is green and the flowers are in bloom, it is a beautiful country. The Pine Ridge Indian Reservation is one of the most scenic places of all. The Bad Lands are the most interesting and mysterious-like of all the Dakota country. But I can't say I saw much beauty on my trip to Pierre.

When I got into town the next day, I started drinking water again and kept it up for four days. I tried beer but never succeeded drinking much as I would get sick on it before I got to feeling foolish. After a few days sitting in the shade and trying to doctor my scorched and bleeding face with vaseline, I started home by way of Fred Fruh's place. Mrs. Fruh, who was a fullblood, and her daughter, Annie, served a good meal without saying a word as the Indian women did, and Fred and I got down to our dominoes.

Things were looking up in the fall and winter of 1899 and 1900. The Boer War in Africa was pushing up the price of horses, and British buyers were in the range country to pick up most anything that looked like a good saddle horse. I bought more horses the next spring, including another stud, and hired Jimmy Hiatt to stay around and herd them. The two studs got along well. They would sort out their own bunches and keep them separate on the range. At night we would put the gray one inside the corral and let the other roam around outside the pen. He would stand at the gate all night and take charge of his harem in the morning.

My neighbor, Rudy, had some real trouble with his horses. He bought a bunch of 216 wild ones, half-mustang and half-Thoroughbred, from a rancher in Greybull, Wyoming. They were as wild as deer and were soon scattered all over the Dakotas, Montana, and Wyoming. A few even went clear back to Graybull. He got tired of chasing these animals all the time and wanted to sell the whole works to Foster and me for fifteen dollars apiece, colts thrown in. We agreed to buy all the stock wearing the BN brand and to pay for what we could round up. Only 150 head were found so we paid him for them, but we owned close to 100 more, including colts, if we could ever find them. As long as Foster and I were in partnership we had an everlasting job chasing these horses. When Foster sold out to me, I fell heir to the job. In the long run, it cost me about twice as much as I ever got out of them. I got some of them from as far away as the South Dakota–Wyoming line. One nice sorrel bronc was caught in 1903 by Frawley Sprague near Slim Butte. He broke him to gentle and sent word for me to come get him.

136

I never took the time to ride halfway across the United States just to get a horse, and I don't know and don't care what Frawley ever did with him. I hope he did him some good.

Foster and I had a job getting the colts of the BN mares branded. They got away in about half the chases, and we wound up with played-out horses in the Fox Ridge or Slim Butte country, forty miles from nowhere, hot, tired, and mostly mad. We would cuss the things and declare we would never chase after them again. Then someone would tell us about a bunch they had seen somewhere and away we would go again.

Once we heard of a bunch on Squaw Creek about one hundred miles west, so we took a pack horse and three good horses apiece and went there. An empty hay corral was fixed up to cut them in, and away we went to find them. That wasn't hard, but to drive them was another matter. These four mares and colts and four slicks with them had been chased so much and let get away they were spoiled. On the Cheyenne River was a rancher who had been in South America. He told us he had chased them many times and he had seen lots of cowpunchers having their turn at them. One morning we sneaked up on them and headed them round and round. We knew we would lose them if we let them run straight away with us behind. This was a bewildering way to run horses, but it worked. In a half hour, with one of us ahead, the other behind, we led them into our corral. They were thinner and smaller than they looked on the range. The small sucking colts had run so much that their ankle joints were puffed up as big as your two doubled fists. The yearlings were sound and nice and built like trim race horses.

While we were at the old hay corral, a flashy-dressed Texas cowhand rode up, looked our camp over, and wanted to know if we owned the branded mares in the pen. Foster told him we did. They argued and nearly quarreled. I told the fellow to get down and eat with us. He said, "No, your stuff don't look fit to eat." We were pretty dirty and our cooking outfit was a mess, but we did not like to hear him say so. While he and Foster cussed and argued, I went to our bed and got out my old Colt revolver, put it on, and kept looking this bluffer in the eye. He finally rode away. That is the way it was; if you got a few slicks in with your own branded stuff, the slow boys hollered.

Our job now was to fix the horses so they could graze and drink but not run. Seeing an old wreck of a mower near the pen, we got four guards off the sickle bar. Each one was about seven inches long and weighed a pound or two. Using an old horse-runner's trick, we threw the old mares and tied one of these guards in the mares' forelocks. If they ran, it would hit them in the forehead or eyes, but if they walked or trotted, it would not swing around and hurt them.

We drove them out in the open and tried it. They started running right away, but when the guards hit them in the head, they would whirl around, rear up and fall back. The colts and yearlings would not leave the mares.

The next morning when we started home, we found two of the colts dead. All of them looked bad. We drove them to Plum Creek that day and let them eat and drink. The next day two of the mares and the other two colts were dead. We got the yearlings and the two old mares to Foster's place the next day and penned them there. All of us, both horses and humans, were pretty gaunt and worn down. Foster took one mare, and I kept the other one. When we trimmed the tails and hocks of the yearlings they looked quite racy. I traded my mare to a trader for a plug saddle horse. Foster tried to halter break his mare but broke her neck. When we heard there was a public horse sale in Pierre, we took the four top yearlings and a few others down and sold them for twelve dollars apiece with the commission out.

This about settled the question of trying to round up the BN brand horses that we had around the country. After fourteen days hard riding, all we had to show for it was forty-eight dollars and six tired saddle horses. Foster declared with a lot of cuss words that he was done. I agreed at the time, but you can't quit chasing wild horses after you start. All you get for it is the sport and experience. Mostly, they get away. Sometimes you can run down a few, and when you do they will fight, bite, and kick. They always look like hundred-dollar horses at a distance with their manes and tails flying. When you get them, they look like a six-dollar piece of wolf bait. Running wild horses is the hardest work that a man can do. You ride forty or fifty miles at a gallop or a run and wind up with a tired horse twenty miles from water or grub. But it is the most interesting sport of all, even if you mostly lose.

CHAPTER 10

SOCIAL LIFE AROUND PIERRE

WHEN I went west in 1890 as a floating laborer, South Dakota was pretty raw and so was I. I first went under the name of Mort, changed it to Wallace DeLong and was called "Walrus," and then back to my real name when I went to Pierre. This was the custom, as so many who went out there were just one jump ahead of the sheriff. Up to that time I had done nothing worse than raiding a watermelon patch, but thought it proper to change my name anyway. I had gone west in the hope of getting wealthy, but after working on the Burlington, carrying a hod at Hot Springs, and running cattle, had decided that this was not the kind of work to get the job done. That's why I turned to horses.

By 1900 the country was pretty well occupied with cattle, horses, and sheep. After the terrible losses of 1896–97, the range was again overstocked and very few ranchers were making any money. The small outfits ran from 50 to 100 cows or 300 to 1,000 sheep, and the big ones ran as high as 5,000. Everybody lived in dugouts or small log houses on springs or creeks and usually had his 160-acre claim fenced as a holding pasture. A few raised some garden stuff. About everybody cut some hay in the summer and had it around the ranch for saddle stock in the winter.

After ten years in South Dakota I had gone up in the world some. I owned a wagon, mower, rake, a twenty-by-twenty log house with a floor, and had 150 horses. At the Pierre bank I owed $1,000. Horses had about doubled in price the last year or two, and my herd nearly doubled every year. Of course, most of my profits were just paper profits as a horse doesn't have much of a sale until it is three or four years old. But anyway, I was doing pretty good.

To do the hard work of riding after strayed broncs and breaking them to lead or to ride, I hired local boys, one or two at a time, like Jimmy Hiatt, Yon Norvald, Jim Jeffries, Jim Jenson, Milt Elkins, Roy Conklin, and Ray Chisholm. All these boys lived on ranches around there and were from eighteen to twenty-two. They did much better at this kind of work than the older cowhands as the old ones would soldier on the job. It was hard work and took a lot of hard, fast riding to pen the snaky ones.

The boys liked to break broncs, and we kept busy at this every spring as we did not have to take time out for two roundups a year the way the cattlemen did. We had a round-up every time some strayed away and went after them and close herded them until they were trained to stay within twenty miles of the ranch. Now and then we would have our own roping and riding contest, and several of the boys around would do their best at riding an unspoiled bronc for the first time. Grubline riders, men hunting for claims, and cowhands looking for work were always coming by and staying for a meal or maybe for a few days. The ranch-raised boys who worked for me could cook, and some of them extra good, so I think we got more than our share of visitors. When I went to Pierre for grub every two or three months, I know I had to bring out quite a wagon load to hold us any time at all.

I took the old *Breeder's Gazette* and the *Weekly Dallas News*, which my boys called the *Bull Journal*, and the *Boll Weevil Journal*. The Texas paper was always complaining of boll weevils, black men, and Republicans. My problem on the Sansarc was Texans. Lots of Texas boys came to Dakota looking for work. A few were from the farming part of Texas and were pretty decent boys, but most of them had malaria or hook worms and looked like scrub stock. I hired one of them once and found him a good, willing worker.

The town of Pierre seemed to draw about all the trash of the East and South, as well as of the West. Seventy-five per cent of the men were steady drinkers and poor providers for their families. Mostly they contented themselves to loaf in the saloons, gamble, and drink when they had the cash. Some of the Pierre folks had jobs in the state capitol, took baths, wore white shirts which they changed once a week, and thought themselves quite aristocratic. The rest of them were common laborers and ranch hands who spent their money as fast as they got it. A tightwad was one who wouldn't spend everything he had, and he was not very popular around there. That description included me.

The women of Pierre were of two kinds, the sporting ladies, as they called themselves, and the wives who tried to raise families decent-like. These decent women didn't venture out much at night alone, and when they did they carried long hat pins or twenty-two revolvers for protection from the drunks. The sporting women were not allowed to recognize their guests on the streets. They didn't have much money as the madams and the pimps took most of it, but they were good spenders in the stores with what they had and so were very welcome. The pimps wore good clothes and, when they were flush, gambled all the time. Mostly they were deadbeats and trash who lived off of the women in the winter and got a ranch job in the summer.

Fort Pierre had no red-light district, but Pierre made up for it. It was big enough to support a woman doctor, who was not patronized by people outside the district. The Fort Pierre people said the girls and madams of the Pierre district were mostly home-talent and an overflow from the divorce colony at Sioux Falls. One of the noted women was Irish Molly. I believe she was one of the first settlers. She lived in a shanty on weedy, brushy Missouri Avenue, and catered to the cheap trade, including Indians, that were not taken at the other houses. She had a boy who was called Irish Tommy. He spent quite a lot of time out at Foster's ranch and later at Narcelle's. But he turned out a convict, shot two people, and was one of a gang that robbed the bank in Fort Pierre where one man was killed.

Nigger Jinny was another one of the women who was not fussy about her business. She was the only Negro in the district and was as big and fat as they came. The old cowhands had dozens of stories about her and the others, most of them not being fit to write about. Once Nigger Jinny was criticized by a drunk cowboy for her kinky hair. She answered, "White man, what do you expect for fifty cents —sealskin?" According to the story, this settled the argument.

An Ottumwa, Iowa, madam had a small house in the district and imported her six or eight girls from home. She had a lady-like manner and was strict with the girls. Only the better element was admitted. Entertainment was provided if the visitors bought beer at one dollar a bottle. Once when one of the girls got reckless in her exhibit as she did the can-can for the men, Maude told her in a shocked and reproving way, "My God, Carrie, be careful. You are showing all you've got." At one time she got a runt of a girl about twenty-five years old, dressed her as a young girl, and told everybody she was her virgin sister and was not to be touched. She kept her in her own room and let a few clients in for twenty-five dollars. A few of the cowhands bit on this swindle. At a roundup near Fort Bennett once, a horse wrangler was telling about this. Old Brigadier General Mark Sheafe, who was there visiting, spoke up and said, "I have heard tall tales, but this is the first time I have ever heard of a cowhand finding a virgin in a whore house." The sporting public soon realized the joke was on them, and the little girl left for other pastures. Old Maud is said to have made a fortune in Pierre and gone back to Ottumwa to spend a respectable old age among her childhood friends.

Jud Matheson had a big frame house and kept eighteen or twenty girls. On the main floor was a good-sized room, big enough for two sets of square dancers at one dollar a dance. It was also expected of the dancers that they tip the piano player, or professor, as he was called. He was an unhealthy looking fellow and probably had V.D. like all the others. Jud and his wife were pretty strict and never let any trouble start at their place.

One of the popular places was run by Old Hallie. She was an ex-show girl of the old free and easy dance and wiggle days, and was past her handsome stage. As she sang her risqué songs and told her coarse jokes, her voice was shrill and sometimes cracked. She had a reputation for putting on a good entertainment and had lots of callers.

The red-light district and the saloons provided about the only entertainment and recreation for the men of that ranch country when I lived there. Most of us were bachelors, not because we wanted to be but because we had to be, and lived pretty lonely lives for weeks or months at a time. Pierre was the place where one could sit in the shade, catch up on the news, and forget some of the hard things of making a living on the prairie. Although I was never one to blow the lid off when I went to Pierre, except for some moderate drinking, I always learned everything of interest that happened among the madams or the gamblers. Most of the people around there were good storytellers even if they couldn't read or write, and these stories were told around every roundup fire or whenever people got together.

One night I went into a restaurant in Pierre and found a bunch of the boys from west of the river there. I knew the first names of most of them. There was Diamond Red, a fellow called Toe Jam, two or three Slims, and about the same number of Shorties. They had heard there was going to be a dance in town and had come in for it. When they learned it was a private dance and had been asked to leave, they were disappointed as they were good dancers according to their ideas. Here they were all dressed up and no place to go. One had used an entire bottle of perfumery, and all had a bottle of whiskey in their pockets. Guns were not allowed in Pierre, so the only weapons they had were knives. The whole bunch was a little noisy when I went into the café. After Diamond Red got into a row with the waiter, we all went outside. Some of the gang thought Red should go back and lick the waiter, but Red didn't want the job. He said the waiter was too big. Everybody encouraged him, saying nobody should get by with what that waiter had said. "Well," said Red finally, "if you all say so, I'll go in and take a licking." We all agreed that in case he got licked the biggest one of us would take the fellow on, and on down to the next biggest until we got him whipped, figuring we could wear him down. Diamond Red took off his coat, fortified himself with several drinks from different bottles, and barged in. We all watched from outside.

Red sat up at the counter and ordered a piece of pie and a cup of coffee. He took his time eating it as we watched. All the time he and the waiter seemed to be talking. When he was done he came on out, said the big jerk inside was a good fellow and would take us all to a place where we could dance. It would cost fifty cents a set but with each set we would get a glass of beer. This sounded good, so we started out as soon as the waiter had closed up the place.

We first went down by Old Hallie's house and the waiter said we should call on her. We knocked at the door and made a lot of noise to get her up as it was pretty late by that time. She lit a lamp and came to the door dressed in a fur coat over a pair of pants belonging to one of her all-night guests. She wanted us to go on as she already had her hands full sleeping with two men. One of the sons of bitches, she said, had got so rough she had given him knock-out drops and she hoped the big stud horse would never wake up. This was a hard life, she complained, and she hoped we would go away now and come back some other time.

Down at Maud Davis's, everything was shut up tight. We hollered and pounded, but no answer, so went on to Jud's place. It was all dark so we hollered and pounded there. He finally opened a little wicket door, told us all the girls had company and he could not get the girls up to dance at that late hour, and shut the door in our face. We were still out and no dance, but nobody spoke up about licking the waiter then.

146

Branding colts on the XO Ranch.
Left to right: Siberts, Joe Hiatt, Ray Chisholm, Jim Jenson.

There was an old barn back of the house, so we went back there to have a few drinks and roll a few cigarets. One fellow prowled the barn and found it had a hog pen attached with an extra-big hog in it. Someone said a poor hog ought not to have to live on the swill from a whore house and that the meat would cause disease. So we turned the hog loose. Then we found a cow in the barn. There was a lot of talk about the cow. Some argued that a nice decent cow should not be kept at a whore house. Some of the boys were pretty full and had a lot to say about a cow's decency, virginity, and other things. It was decided to rescue the cow from this life of shame as a whore house cow, so they took off her bell and led her away.

Everything but the depot was dark as we went back to town. We tied the cow to a hitch rack and went inside the depot to get warm. After we got warm, we decided to have a stag dance ourselves as two of the boys had mouth organs. While they played, one rang the cowbell and another pounded the poker on the stove. It was a lively dance with a lot of noise and jumping around. The night operator finally opened the ticket window and told us to quit banging the poker on the stove as we would break it. But we kept on for about two hours. When two women came in to take the early train east, the agent said the dance was over and we left.

We still had the cow, and so we took her along while we looked for a place to sleep. Some wanted to find a quiet buyer for her, but after a long argument we decided to turn her loose. She left on a trot for the old barn, and we still had the bell and the rope. We knew the hotels wouldn't let us in even if they weren't full, so we went to the livery barn. We prowled around and found an empty box stall so we got hay, found an old tarpaulin and some smelly horse blankets, and settled down for the night. I wanted to go to my room in the hotel, but the gang would not let me as they knew I owned a checkbook which would be mighty handy if we found ourselves in a jam. When the bunch got to snoring good, I sneaked out and went to the hotel as I knew how to get in through the kitchen. My partner, McGaff, was taking his eighty acres right in the middle of the bed and he woke up and asked me what time it was. I told him it was half-past ten and not to forget it. "Oh," he said, "you want an alibi. What is the crime, rape or horse-stealing?" I told him it was both and that murder would be added if he forgot that I got in at half-past ten. He said, "All right," and went back to sleep.

I saw Diamond Red some days later, and he told me how the livery-barn man had jawed them for sleeping in the box stall and had made them pay one dollar for the night. They had taken the cowbell and rope across the river to a sheep-herder and told him old Jud would let him sleep with one of the girls if he returned them. Diamond Red never heard how he came out.

When I was in the barber shop, one of the barbers told me how a gang of outlaws from Fort Pierre had come into town, stole some hogs and cows, and raised quite a disturbance at the depot. There was some pretty fierce talk about the whole matter. I agreed that the Fort Pierre toughs were pretty bad, but I didn't say much more than that. I had a pretty good reputation in Pierre and wanted to keep it.

The cowhands and sheepherders spent most of their lives out on the prairie and seldom got into town to get in scrapes as I nearly did that time. Most of them had either grown up out there somewhere or came from the settled country not far back. A lot of people over fifty and a lot of the young men who grew up around Pierre couldn't read or write, and their heads were pretty empty. I guess all of them had a religion of some kind, but it dealt with hell-fire and damnation mostly, as they had got it from preachers who couldn't read or write any better than they could. A few of the old cowhands had some pretty funny ideas on religion. They claimed that after an old cowhand died he came back to the prairie as a jack rabbit and that to shoot one would be murder. Unless these rabbits were shot by some bad person or until some animal killed them, they lived forever. Once at a roundup we were arguing religion when a storm came up and lightning struck the cook's Dutch oven and scattered the pots and pans all around. This made the cook so mad he shook his fist toward the sky and said, "Raise your sights, you old bald-headed son of a bitch, if you want to get me." The other men were scared and ran all over the prairie. One said, "The Old Man will get him next crack. You will see. He shouldn't have said what he did." Some of these people spoke of "Old Johnny God" as a big bald man with whiskers who had quite a temper and might strike a man dead if he did wrong. Of course, with a few drinks in them, they didn't worry too much about it.

CHAPTER 11

RANGE LIFE AND CUSTOMS
IN THE WINTER OF 1900–1901

I N OCTOBER, 1900, I was in Pierre to get some grub and saw
Ed Lyman, a half-breed, who was Narceese Narcelle's
wagon boss. As they had just finished loading their last of a
ten-car beef shipment, I asked him if he had seen any of my
BN horses up on the reservation where they ran their stuff.
I told him Foster and I were out about 150 head of the broncs
we had bought from Rudy and that I was going to ride up
in that country to look for them. He said Narcelle didn't
want me to ride his range or use his pens and made quite a
bluff until I told him I rode where I wanted to. Then he said

they were going to round up their horses soon and that I could come and join them. I checked with Diamond Red, the cook of the Narcelle wagon, and he told me they had seen a lot of BN stock during the beef roundup. My mind was made up.

I got my horses ready, left Herb Howland at the ranch, and in about ten days left for the Fox Ridge and Slim Buttes country. At noon I had dinner with Doug Carlin, and he advised me not to go as old Narcelle did not like me and I might get into trouble. I went on to the Leslie store and post office and stayed with Jim Benteen who ran it. That night Benteen tried to get me to turn around as he knew old Narcelle had a bad heart. Ed Jones, who was there, told me to go on. He said they tried to talk him out of riding the Narcelle range but he had gone anyway and found out it was all a bluff. For ten years I had heard so many tales like this that they no longer bothered me.

At Robinson's store at the Cherry Creek subagency I got a lot of Bull Durham and more free advice and went on. After eating dinner with an old Indian called Widow, I got to Narcelle's ranch and found Diamond Red and Water Crackers, the day wrangler, on hand to meet me. Ed Lyman was a little grumpy as usual. The next day a fellow called Poor Boy came in with a string of fresh horses from Moreau River and the roundup was ready to begin. We had a crew of four whites, a few half-breeds, and several fullbloods. No wonder Diamond Red said he was glad I was there as he got so lonesome for white folks.

Two Indians had been sent out earlier to fix up the pens and to get the camp ready. They had a big twelve-by-twenty-four tent set up over a mess box so we could eat and sleep under it. Diamond Red told me and Poor Boy not to use the regular towel made of a two-bushel canvas sack as all the Indians had sore eyes and some had a tuberculosis cough.

He put out a special one for us. The word sanitary was not yet known in Dakota. Sometimes roundup towels got so stale that some of us would use our shirttail instead. Generally the Indians had little to do with us. They were quiet and seemed sullen but were probably just a little scared of white men. Most of the old cowhands were mean to fullbloods and called them gut-eaters and other names. Poor Boy and I bedded down together in the back of the tent and got along fine.

We got up early the next morning, ate breakfast by lantern light, and as soon as the night hawk had the horses in the rope corral, we saddled up and followed Lyman toward Eagle Butte. He scattered us along, and Poor Boy was to lead seven or eight of us south on a half-circle of about twenty-five miles while Lyman was to take the north circle. We started a lot of very wild ones that were soon out of sight leaving clouds of dust. The Narcelle bunches were not so wild. About one o'clock, the circles met and we had 600 horses to turn over to the two day herders. The cattle were so thick on this range that Ed decided to hold a cattle roundup and drive them west. The next day we got between 3,000 and 4,000 wearing all kinds of brands but mostly Texas stock and drove them about fifteen miles west. Three Indians were given some grub and a blanket and told to push them along until dark and then drive them all the next day. The boys came back in four days and said they had driven them west of Castle Buttes and the dogies were still going west on a trot. These cattle had been trespassing on the reservation, but the boys had put them at least fifty miles beyond the line.

At the end of the second day's horse roundup we had about 1,000 head and had let a lot of wild ones get away. Ed changed his plan and decided to put the day herd on a big hill and let them scatter some. Then we made a circle leaving two men on each side of where the horses were to come from. This was to keep them from turning back and out-running the ones that started them. Poor Boy and I had one side on a high butte. It was cold so we changed off. One would go down where there was a little wood, make a fire, and warm up a half-hour, then go and spell the other one while he went down. When the wild horses would come in sight, the man on the butte would wave his hat and the run would start to keep them headed towards the day herd. This took a run of six or seven miles. After we got them in the big bunch, the herders would mill them some, and most of them would stay in the middle. A few would go on through the herd and get away after a lot of running and leave a couple of played-out horses. The Indian boys liked to run them and would keep at it until their horses quit. The little white mare with red ears came in with her bunch and we had to chase her a lot before we got her back and milled her. It would have been right to shoot her, but she was really a good looker. We finally penned her bunch and gagged her so she couldn't eat or drink for two days. She was all right for a while after we put her in the big herd again, but one day she made her break, and the day herders had to let her go. All in all, we let about 5 per cent escape.

One day we took extra horses and went north to Moreau River. We camped with a hay outfit. They had corrals and were going to wean calves and feed poor cows for some out-fit. We stayed all night and had lots to eat. The fresh-killed beef was good, but I didn't see any hide on the corral fence. We had manners, so we made no comment. The next day we rode to Thunder Butte and Slim Buttes where we saw a lot of horses and cattle as well as prairie and sky. We gathered quite a bunch of stock, cleaned out of it what we wanted, including three of mine, and came on to the pens by way of the hay camp.

That night Diamond Red and Water Crackers had a big

row. Red got him down and was slapping him. When I yelled at Red to get off, he jumped up, ran to the mess box after a butcher knife, and was going to cut Water Crackers' throat. Water Crackers got a stove lid, threw it at Red, but missed him and hit me on the shin. At that time Lyman took charge and told them to quit. I pulled off my boot and my shin was bloody and it hurt like blazes. Everybody thought it was a good joke that I was the only casualty after all the bad language and fighting. The battle was over, and Water Crackers and Red slept together that night.

We cleaned out our herd the next morning and started to Narcelle's with about 1,600 horses. As we went down a long ridge, an old mare and her six colts tried to make a get away. An Indian boy tried to head them off on his played-out horse but he couldn't outrun them. I started out on my fresh horse and caught up with them in a little valley four or five miles away. The old mare was all in. I took down my rope and was ready to double it and whip her with it when she turned and charged me. With her mouth open and ears laid back, she bore down on me and tried to bite my leg, but got hold of the cantle of the saddle. I swung my horse and her teeth snapped together as her grip slipped. At two hundred yards I stopped and looked back. She looked at me. I could see that she had been run so much that she had bad joints and most of the colts were in the same condition. Since the bunch wasn't worth driving home, I left the spavin-legged old rip standing there and went on over the ridge.

It was good to get in a good log house again that night, eat at a table, and sleep in a bunkhouse with a stove in it. The Indian boys went down to see their girls after supper, and Ed Lyman went home to his family. Narcelle's book-keeper, Jimmy, was there, so he and I played cards, talked, and even tried a few songs. The night hawk stayed on his job even if the horses were penned. He sure earned his thirty dollars a month pay riding herd on cold November nights like that one.

A rider from Moreau Creek came in the next day and helped Poor Boy cut out about one hundred horses that belonged in that country and started home with them. I helped brand and castrate the rest of the day and the following morning started home with my string of eight broncs. Three of the wild fillies were pretty snaky so Water Crackers helped me for five or six miles. When he had to go back, we penned them in an Indian corral and I hired a young full-blood to go on from there. We ran them for the first six or seven miles as we started on, and then they settled down to a steady trot. At Leslie we watered the stock and put them in a cow corral. A lot of Indians were camped there, and the boy found some of his cousins. I gave him two dollars, and he said he was going to stay there awhile and spend his money.

I rode over to the store and found out they were getting ready for a dance. A lot of wagons, buckboards, and saddle horses were around, and inside I saw a number of girls and young married women all dressed up. The men were getting started on the drinking end of the dance, and a poker game was going on. I had three-weeks' growth of whiskers and my clothes were pretty dirty, but I stayed on to be a wall flower or weed. There were more stags than women, so they would lie across the beds in the bunkhouse waiting their turn. Each set cost fifty cents, the money going to the fiddlers. After watching the dancing and poker playing for a while, I crawled in a bunk with a young fellow who had celebrated too much. Later on, a young Indian called Eddie Swan, who weighed 225 pounds, came to bed with us without taking off his boots, spurs, or anything else. It was a little too crowded and the bed sagged nearly to the floor. We fixed a quilt on the floor and rolled him off on it, and he never

155

knew anything about it until morning. The rest of the people started leaving by two o'clock but a few were still there when I got up and had breakfast the next morning.

After selling my three wild fillies to Ed Jones for sixty dollars, I went on home. Herb Howland said he had been having a good time, doing nothing but hauling wood and cooking for the passers-by. I fixed up the clothes line and hung my bed and all my clothes out to air. I wanted to be sure I had not picked up what we called a batch of crumbs. After shaving and cleaning up, it seemed awful good to be back on the white side of the river. While I read the weekly papers and rested, Herb went to Lindsay Post Office to visit and to see an Indian girl he was sweet on across the river. I checked on some of my horses and found them a lot more tame than the Fox Ridge bunches. The stallions herded their own bands well, and the colts were coming along. The wolves would kill one now and then, but we shot them or trapped them and kept them down. The horse business was paying off, and a good horse was now worth from thirty-five to sixty dollars. I was doing all right even if I never found a one of the 150 BN broncs roaming the country somewhere west of the Mississippi and east of the Rocky Mountains.

After the colts were branded in the fall of 1900, I took the buggy team and went to pay Ed Dupree a visit. Ed had been born around Civil War time near Fort Sully, where Fred, his father, had a trading store. When the Texas trail drivers came up to the post with a herd of cattle, they would let old Fred have the calves. This started him in the cattle business, and by the time I knew him he had thousands of horses and cattle and a lot of half-breed children and relatives who lived at the home ranch on the reservation. When there is a death in an Indian family, it is customary to give away a lot of the property. The children started to give twenty-dollar gold pieces and stock to all the Indians and whites who gathered there when Fred died, but Doug Carlin made them stop. At another time a bunch of Crow Indians came from Montana on a visit. Several cattle were killed to feed them, and then they rigged up an extra-good saddle horse and placed on it two hundred silver dollars. Every Indian walked by the horse and picked off a dollar, the last one getting the bronc himself. In this way, Dupree's estate was soon scattered and gone.

Ed lived about thirty-five miles from me up Cheyenne River and across Fox Ridge. He was doing pretty well. When I got there at dusk, he came out to welcome me. He had stopped at my place a lot of times when on the way to Pierre, so we were good friends. He had his Indian cowhands unhitch my team, and we went on into the house. In most of the Indian camps, the women stayed in the kitchen and maybe the men would never see them. Ed's wife, Mary, was different. She was a half-breed but had been a schoolteacher. While Ed talked a mixture of Indian, French, and English all at one time, she could talk any one of them separately. While a girl did the cooking, Mary ate at the table with Ed and me. She was lonesome living so far away from any of her own people and wanted to know all the news of the people south of the Cheyenne. When we went into another room after supper for some whiskey and cigarets, she went back to the kitchen.

Ed wanted me to stay longer, but after a day and two nights I decided to get back to the Sansarc. On the way I saw a big bunch of horses. They seemed pretty quiet, so I drove around them to see if I might not find one of my BN broncs. Sure enough, I did see a good one of mine, and as the bunch was tame I thought I would try to herd them along and put them in Rudy's pen. There I could catch the bronc and take him home with me. It was a job to drive them with a team and buggy. When I got them near the pen, they changed their minds and galloped back on me. I tried it again, but it was no good. In going across a small draw, I nearly upset and decided to give it up as a bad job. It was late afternoon, the team was tired, and I was thirty miles from home, so I decided to stay at Rudy's dugout that night. I was cold and discouraged with myself for being such a fool.

A dugout is about the worst-looking kind of a house that can be found anywhere, but it is fine in a pinch. Rudy's place looked desolate there in the middle of the prairies, but I was in a pinch so tied my team and went in to see about bedding down there. When I lit the candle and got a fire going, it looked better. The grub box had baking powder, salt pork, coffee, and beans in it, enough for a real meal. I got out the ax and chopped through a foot of ice to water the team before I put them in the hay corral for the night. After getting the place warm and eating my supper of sow belly and biscuits, I pulled off my cold leather boots and got comfortable. Felt boots are warm but not very nifty looking so I had worn the leather ones to impress the Duprees. After I rolled a cigaret, I looked over Rudy's books. He was a Princeton man and had Marcus Aurelius, Dickens, and Boccaccio to read when he was there alone. I picked Boccaccio and pretty nearly forgot to go to bed that night.

By morning a blizzard had moved in on Dakota, so I holed up until it blew over. When I watered the horses and brought in a coffeepot full of water, I saw cattle drifting into an ash grove down in the draw. This gave me an idea as to how to improve my standard of living. I got out my old revolver and Rudy's butcher knife and went down creek. Mostly they were Dupree cattle, but when I saw a Shorthorn cow and calf wearing a foreign brand, I knew I had solved my problem. The old cow was thin and the calf was still sucking so I decided to save the mother's life by butchering the calf. Besides, the Wyoming Stock Association owed me for a big roan steer which they had shipped in 1893 and put the proceeds in the stray account. In the seven years I had collected some on the debt now and then, and now decided to pick up a little interest. The calf weighed four hundred pounds and made good eating. The coyotes cleaned up the offal, and I saved the hide as it had no brand on it yet. The old Shorthorn did a lot of bawling over the loss of her calf, so I gave her some hay and milked her to make her feel better. Eating Wyoming beef made me feel better, too, even if I didn't give thanks over it. One time a very religious sheepman killed an extra fine O.P. calf and at the first meal was saying grace. He took so long that the herders started eating before he said "amen." When he saw them sin that way, he dressed them down and reckoned their chances of salvation were not much good.

I stayed there in the dugout for four days eating beef and reading books. I thought Marcus Aurelius had thought a lot of things out pretty well, but I liked Boccaccio better. After reading both of them, I was ready to go home and enter Pierre society about any place there was an opening. Even the girls who were on the "touch me not" order seemed powerful interesting to me as I read this literature. When the blizzard passed, I hung up a quarter of the beef on the ridge pole for some other passer-by, washed my dishes, warmed up the bridle bits, hitched up, and started home. I stopped at Foster's to warm up and give him some beef, and got in that night. Herb was pretty glad to see me after a week of talking to himself. After he had eaten some beefsteak and heard about Boccaccio, he brightened up quite a bit.

In February two of the neighbor boys wanted me to help them kill some fresh beef. They knew where a black, muley Angus and her heifer were hanging out five miles northwest of my place and wanted me to meet them there. I sharpened my butcher knife and took my Winchester and rode out there. The boys cut out the heifer instead of driving the herd over, so I had to shoot the heifer on the run. We dressed it on the hide, split the backbone with an ax, and were done in no time. I took a quarter along as my part of the swag.

As long as I lived in Stanley County, killing one's own beef was not considered the thing to do. I know of only one case for certain and that was an accident. A man I'd better just call John was camped with another rancher named Harvey. John was a tightwad and Harvey was a practical joker and a liar. Once Harvey told his partner they would kill a good fat O.P. beef at night and burn the hide so they wouldn't run any risk at all. That night they killed the cow and were butchering her before a big fire when some of Harvey's friends, unknown to John, rode out of the dark and pretended to be the owners of the brand. They threatened arrest, jail, and even the pen, and scared John so bad he wrote a check for $100 to pay the damages. Later Harvey and his conspirators went to Pierre and had a wonderful time in the saloons and sporting houses with the money. Of course, the tale leaked out, and Tightwad John was a dangerous man to be around for quite awhile.

Two college men, Morton and Whiteside, started to build a cabin on the Cheyenne bottom in the spring of 1901. They got the walls up and then left for town to get grub. While they were gone, a big cattle outfit started to build down the river from them and stole all the logs that the college boys had piled up at their place. When they got back from town, they did not know what to do so came around to the little ranchers to ask advice. We offered to go with them and take the logs out of the completed house of the thieves. They were afraid to do that. While we were chewing the rag, we decided to kill one of the big outfit's beeves, and were eating it when the boss came up. He wanted to know what the hell we were doing. We told him to get down and eat some of this good meat. He rode off and that was the end of the party, but not of other people eating his beef.

Most of the ranchers killed three or four beeves every winter and lived mostly on bacon and salt meat in the summer. When we butchered in the warm months, we usually cut off a quarter for a neighbor and one's self and left the rest to the coyotes. It was very wasteful, besides the calf meat was rich and gave one bowel trouble and cramps. Sometimes we put up veal in a barrel of brine that would float a potato and then added saltpeter. This could be kept in a cool place for several months. We had the general idea that our sex hunger was caused by such a heavy meat diet, but I never heard of anyone going vegetarian because of this.

Winter in a log cabin, even with a board floor, is not an exciting life. Herb and I hauled wood from the draw on the Sansarc, went after the mail once a week, and read the old *Bull Journals* again. The snow on the ground kept the horses from wandering far and the grass that they pawed for gave them enough moisture so we didn't have to chop ice-holes in the river. It was so quiet that I decided to go to Fort Pierre to try town life awhile.

The snow made it hard riding but I made it to Meer's Road Ranch by dark that night. The boy who brought the lantern out to help me take care of my horse told me supper was over and the cook, Grindstone Annie, might not be in good humor, but to talk nice to her and she might fire up the stove again. I went in and asked her as polite as I could, and she said, "Why, you poor child, I will feed you all you can hold." While she warmed my supper and baked pies for the next day, she told me she was from the Ozarks and had been

cooking in mining camps, lumber camps, and boarding-
houses in Deadwood and Scooptown (Sturgis) for twenty
years. She was forty-five and weighed about 120 pounds. I
asked her if she had even been married. "Well, yes, once by
law, but the son of a bitch would not work and finally run
off with a poxy whore." She was glad to get rid of him and
it had served him right. She had not bothered to get married
again but had lived with several men, mostly no good tinhorn gamblers, one or two at a time but not long with any
one of them.

One of her men had been a traveling preacher. He had
first been a Bible peddler, but had got to be a pretty good
spieler on religion and had got to be a holy man who could
conduct funerals and marry people. Besides that, he never
worked much after living with her, but would eat off of the
people she worked for. She liked him good at first, but he
played hooky on her when he could find a pushover. She
always slept in the kitchen as it was handy to get up and
start breakfast, but because the drunks would try to come
see her at night, she kept the kitchen door locked. The
preacher slept down the hall in this boardinghouse where
she worked and would come knock at the door when he
wanted in. One night he knocked, and as she was tired, she
told him to go on back to his room. He kept tapping but
finally got mad at having to stand in the cold hall and went
back to bed. This started family trouble. One night she
packed, boarded a late stage for Cheyenne, and never saw
him again.

All of these adventures were told in a very frank style
with the old four-letter words and a lot of detail. She talked
of sex as some would talk of weather, said she had been hot
blooded once, but now had sex life only as an accommodation for friends. I listened for over two hours and thanked
her for her extra work. She gave me some advice about avoid-

Siberts at the XO Ranch, 1906

ing some of the various bad women and told me to come see her when I got my clean clothes on. I bid her good night and good luck.

The twenty-five miles to Fort Pierre was a long cold one. The road was broke and there were quite a few travelers with red noses going both ways. After putting my horse in Dave Crippen's livery for thirty cents a night, I had beefsteak, eggs, and potatoes for supper. After that I went to a saloon and ordered whiskey. Several of the old rounders came up, and I set them up for them, laid down two dollars on the bar and told the bartender to keep the change. That was a good way to leave the bar flies. I rode a hack across the ice to Pierre for fifteen cents and went to the old Northwestern Hotel and found John McGaff, one of my old friends, who had a ranch on Plum Creek.

We loafed around in the lobby and saw a lot of people. One was a woman who was getting a divorce from a good provider and who was living with a gambler. She said this new man of hers had a sure thing when he toured the county fairs with a wheel of fortune but had lost his $2,500 stake to the professionals in Pierre. He had sold his watch and clothes but had still lost. Then he stole an overcoat and got caught at it. The marshal had taken him down the tracks about five miles and told him to hit the ties and never come back. Now he was dead broke, and his girl-friend worked as a waitress. It was a hard life, she said, and we agreed.

One guest of the hotel had a bad case of pox. It was very offensive, and as all people used the same lavatory with two bowls and a roller towel, it caused complaints. The proprietor finally put him out after a lot of argument, burned the towel, and disinfected the lavatory. One barbershop adopted the name of Sanitary Shop and kept the razors sterilized in a solution of carbolic acid. Some of the legislators began to talk about an antispitting law.

163

Pierre was quite a town when the legislature was in session. The legislators were mostly country lawyers and windy
farmers, with Scandinavians in the majority. The politics
were of the old Republican style—to the victors belong the
spoils, mostly by robbing themselves. They spent quite a
lot of time that winter adopting a state flower and a wolf
bounty, but they had plenty of time to chase chippies, get
drunk, and go down the line on old Missouri Avenue. The
state printer made a good thing of his contract to publish the
proceedings at so much a line. He printed it this way when
he could:

And
The
Bill
Passed

THESE cheap politicians had all-year-round passes on the
North Western and the Milwaukee railroads. Any voter
could get one of these from his representative or the lobby-
ists. Two of the guests at the hotel had got passes for themselves to go to Clark on Sunday and offered to get them for
anybody else who wanted to go. I went along just to have
something to do. We stayed in a hotel in Clark and spent
most of the time playing cards. Some of the local folks tried
to sell us town lots as they believed the town would soon be
a large city. The rain belt was moving west, and it would
soon be a wheat country. But for me, one Sunday there was
enough. We left on the Monday morning train and after
a slow ride got back Tuesday afternoon. Pierre sure looked
good after a week-end in the wheat country.

A show troop had moved into the hotel while we were
gone. Some of the girls said they had played all the way
from New York to Pierre and while they had been stranded

a few times had never had to walk. They were mostly sociable but on the gold-digging side. A few of the dancers were
suffering from corns. The men in the troop wore Hart,
Schaffner and Marx suits that cost about eighteen dollars so
must have been prosperous sometime. This life looked hard
but a little romantic to me then. The thing that got me was
how wilted and old the girls looked when they came down
to a late breakfast about noon. We were sorry to see them
move on to the Black Hills after their two weeks' stand with
us.

CHAPTER 12

CHASING RUSTLERS AND RATTLERS

WHILE I was in Pierre learning how the government was run, I got a message from Foster telling me to come at once as some of the Indians and half-breeds were stealing our horses and driving them across the Cheyenne. He was tied down with his sheep and wanted me to get a Winchester and a lot of cartridges and start out right away.

I started out facing a cold wind and got the full force of it with my clean shave and haircut town style. That night I stayed at Fred Fruh's good log house on the Missouri and learned he had heard of the horse-stealing. He wanted me to look out for about one hundred of his brand which he thought were gone, and wrote me an order to take his horses anywhere at his expense. That would protect me from the charge of stealing if I should find them. I think old Fred was such a good friend of mine because both he and my father were Civil War veterans.

When I got home, Herb rode over to Foster's sheep camp to get him. By midnight they were back, and we talked the rest of the night. He told me the gang had changed our Y brand into an 8, but it would be easy to detect it as a fresh burn on a winter coat would show plain. All the ranchers around were worried and wanted me to do the riding for them, they to furnish the horses and pay the expenses. Several offered me their Winchesters, and if I could shoot the red sons of bitches, they would see that I didn't get hung for it. I agreed to go hunt the stock, but on the killing, I said the old rule would apply, every man should kill his own snakes. These old boys were in the habit of threatening to kill most anybody, but most of them could not hit a rabbit setting still at ten feet.

The next day I started out riding one horse and leading another and headed up the Cheyenne River. Not far from Pete Dupree's ranch I caught up with a big young Indian riding a gray bronc with the Y brand burned into an 8. I told him to get off and held my old Colt forty-one calibre on him. He was so scared he turned a dirty gray color, and while I sat on my horse he took his saddle off and put a rope around the horse's neck. I left him standing there while I moved on with the horse to Dupree's. Both Frank and Pete were there to see the worked-over brand. Frank said there were a few more around and for me to go to the Cherry Creek agency where a crowd of Indians had gathered to draw their monthly beef rations.

I went on up the river, stopped for dinner at Carlin's,

and on to Benteen's Road Ranch where I stayed that night. The ranchers who were there drinking that evening got excited about this brand-burning and everybody thought they had lost some too. A good many of them just gathered their horses in the spring, branded the colts and castrated the yearlings, and after taking out some to break, turned them loose again. Any thief could have made off with horses, and unless seen by someone, the owner would not know of it for a long time.

At Benteen's I crossed the river on the ice. People had put dirt and sand on the slick parts so horses wouldn't fall. About five hundred Indians were camped at the subagency, and there were wagons and tepees all over the place. I rode around the camp and found two more of my broncs with the blotched brands picketed among the ponies. After taking off the saddles and bridles, I started toward Benteen's again with my stock. Two Indian police watched me all the time, but they didn't do anything as they no doubt had heard all about the horse-stealing by the grapevine telegraph. By sundown the next day I was home with my three broncs.

At Lindsay Post Office the next day I saw Bull Marshall, a half-breed who hung around there a lot. He told me that two young Indians from Standing Rock agency at Fort Yates just across the line in North Dakota had done this stealing. Three of the local boys had helped and had got a bronc apiece for their share. The Standing Rock pair had taken twenty of the Y-brand horses north, one riding one of my XO saddle mares and the other one of Foster's. The trail to Standing Rock would be easy to follow, so I decided to beard the red devils in their den.

I caught up a fresh saddle horse and another to pack my bed and grub on, and started north. The first night I stayed in a dugout on Abear Creek and the next at a horse corral on Virgin Creek. Wood was scarce and the ice was two feet thick on the creek. It was cold making camp in the washout hole, but it was warm sleeping with my clothes on under a buffalo robe. There were a lot of stock and a few wolves and coyotes around. After eating left-over flapjacks and bacon the next morning, I went on north across Moreau Creek and found a good-looking log house. A fullblood came out and just stood there. I told him what I was looking for by signs and marking on the ground. He understood and pointed north with his chin and said, "One sleep." I gave him a sack of Bull Durham and some papers, looked at the sun, and pointed to his house. He said, "How," which means "good," as well as several other things. A boy came out when he hollered, took my horses to water, unsaddled them, and put them in the hay corral.

The house was neat and clean. The woman fed the old man and me first, giving us bread and coffee, Indian style with the sugar cooked in it. Then we went into the other room and smoked. He lit his pipe as Indians always do with a stick held in the stove until it blazes. I talked mostly English and he talked Sioux, but we got along pretty well. I learned his people were of the Bull tribe, so called because of their roan bull color. He drew a map on the dirt floor and marked the spot about five miles north of Fort Yates where I could find the horse thieves.

After a good sleep on the floor covered with quilts and blankets. I got out early and was on the trail north. The few Indians I met on horses or in Government Issue Democrat wagons were surly and never even raised a hand or spoke to me. I tried to ask about my horses, but they would just spit, look mean, and not answer. This sure didn't make the trip any more interesting to me.

The fort had been abandoned by the army, but the agent's office was there. I found some Indian police and made them understand that I wanted to feed my horses and stay all night. One took me to a barn where I watered and fed my horses. There was no chance to eat, he told me, as the trading store was closed. I never let on I was hungry but followed him to a sort of office where he slept, unrolled my bed which was getting to smell of sweat, and got out my last cold flapjack for my supper.

In the morning I went to the store, got some sardines and crackers, and had a good meal before a red-hot stove. Then I went to the agent's office and told him and the Indian police what I was there for. He sent one of them out and in about an hour he came back and said, "Come." We rode north on a trail two miles until we came to a cabin. Smoke was coming out of the chimney, but the place was shut tight and no one came out. In a round corral back of the cabin were twenty-one of the Y horses with their brands blotched into an 8. We drove them back to the agency, where I reported to the agent. He advised me to go around the Indian reservations on the way back even if it was two hundred miles, so I packed my bedroll and started back with my jaded broncs.

My trail home was through a white man's country. Around Pollack there were farms raising wheat and small grain. The grade for a railroad had been made and some fair looking shacks made up the town. I got feed for my horses for $3.75 and had some good meals in the hotel. At Selby two days later, the sheriff looked me over pretty careful like. I not only had two weeks of whiskers but had twenty-one horses with blotched brands. Before he would let me go he wired Bert Cummins of the First National Bank of Pierre, and Bert wired back that I was all right and asked them to cash my check. I decided to rest there a few days.

When it was noised around that I could cash checks, I became a sort of man of distinction. I bought new corduroy pants, a shirt, underwear, and jacket, and took them to the barbershop where I got shaved and had a twenty-five-cent bath in the tub. The schoolteacher who ate in the hotel had turned up her nose at me until I got cleaned up. After that, she was very friendly and invited me to her rooming house. We sat in the parlor together every night I was there. The widow who ran the place was a pest. She would go through the room and make remarks about when we were going to get married, what we were going to name the baby, and then laugh at her own cracks. One afternoon the widow invited me to her house for a piece of fresh-baked pie. I went over and had a good time. After this, I spent the afternoons with her and the evenings with the schoolma'm. The widow knew it was all nonsense and would remark, "I don't know what makes me so foolish." I'm sure I didn't know. It seems a common trait of human beings. Maybe a gentleman shouldn't tell secrets, anyway.

My horses were in fair shape after ten days' rest, so after buying another saddle horse for thirty-five dollars, I closed up my social affairs with the schoolma'm and the widow and started home. That night I stayed at a farmhouse with a young couple and turned my stock in their pasture. These people had been raising small grain and had done well, but wanted to go west of the river and raise cattle. After spending a night in the one-dollar hotels of Gettysburg and another little town, I got to Pierre. There I sold my thirty-five-dollar bronc for sixty dollars and hired a boy, Joe Perry, to go home with me until spring work started. It felt good to be on the west side of the Missouri again as we started home. That night we put the broncs in the pasture at Hopkins' Road Ranch for a nickel apiece. The next day we trotted them along and were home at noon.

Besides the hard work of riding in sub-zero weather, the trip had cost me ninety dollars. Foster paid this as his share of the cost. I had a profit of twenty-five dollars on the saddle

171

horse I sold in Pierre. The trip had this other advantage: It helped my reputation around when people knew I would go deep into the Indian country and get my stolen horses rather than let somebody get by with something. Some had predicted I would never get back alive. Maybe there was a little hope in this as many people did not like me overmuch. When I told about my trip, I spread it on a bit and some of the stories stuck.

As a horse rancher I was doing pretty well at my XO place on the Sansarc. I had between four and five hundred broncs, mostly paid for, and was making some money at least on paper. We gathered the strayed mares in the spring and herded them in my holding pasture and turned them out in the morning. The five gray stallions would sort their harems out and watch over them all day long. It wasn't hard to keep track of them this way. Now and then a wolf would kill a colt, but they made themselves pretty scarce as we kept a Winchester on our saddle, and we dusted them off whenever we could get a shot. The neighbor boys who worked for me helped me break broncs and ride herd, and this made life a lot easier than when I had to go it alone.

But it wasn't all work and no play. Killing snakes was one of our pastimes and we always got off and hit them with a rope when we saw them around. Sometimes in the summer we found them in the house. That spring of 1902 we found a whole mess of them east of the ranch about two miles. A high bluff had caved in, leaving a big crack about three feet wide and thirty feet deep. There were a lot of rattlers at the bottom. We got some trash, set it afire, and dropped it in. The snakes sure worked their rattles overtime then. One of the boys said we ought to let one of us down on a rope and he could club them to death, but everybody wanted the other fellow to go down. I went to the cabin and got a shotgun and a rifle, and we fired several shots into the snakes, making them do some more rattling and squirming. We got a jug of kerosene and after soaking up some old rags, poured it down the pit, dropped in some blasting powder, poked in the burning rags, and ran. The whole mess went off with a dull boom. It rained snakes and dirt all over us. We got clubs and started in killing snakes and soon had about one hundred bunched up. The next day we went back, killed a few more, and after pouring kerosene on them, and setting them afire, pushed the whole works into the hole and threw dirt on them. It was sure a good snake-killing.

One day when I got back from Lindsay Post Office, Jimmy Hiatt met me at the corral and said we had trouble in the house. An old cowhand called Lucky Bill, who was both locoed and drunk, was making a nuisance of himself inside. He was broke and had come on a horse he didn't own, which he had turned loose to go home. When I went in, he was on the bunk and was pretty surly. He had stopped at Lindsay and had bought a dozen bottles of lemon extract. Now he was half-drunk and sick on this poisonous mixture which a lot of old sots used as a last resort. When he wanted to borrow twenty-five dollars and start a poker game I told him no, pretty short. He got out his old six-shooter, went outdoors to shoot off a box of shells, and came back in and drank another five or six bottles of extract mixed with sugar and water. This quieted him and he went to sleep. The boys thought maybe we had better kill him, but decided not to on account of the law against murder. Besides he hadn't done anything but talk mean.

We always kept visitors as long as they wanted to stay, but the ones that hung around for a day or two always helped cook and do any other work at hand. After Lucky Bill got over his drunk, he wanted to show us how to break broncs. We picked out a mean one and told him he could have it to ride as long as he stayed. He put a hackamore on the bronc, tied up one foot, threw a saddle on, and let it buck. Then he blindfolded it, tied the hackamore rope to the saddle horn so the horse wouldn't get his head down, and got on. The bronc could only crow-hop. He knew how to take advantage of a bad one. We got along pretty well with him after that.

I went to Lindsay to get the mail and to look around for some horses that had wandered over that way. When I came back a couple of days later, Lucky Bill was gone. He had run in a bunch of strays and had taken a team of broke horses out of it, packed his war bag and a big lunch, lifted my razor and shaving kit, and high-tailed it out of the country. We heard afterward he had gone south to Bad River, where he had sold one of the horses and bought some Jamaica ginger. After going to a ranch around there, he had filled up on Jake and died. The cowhands tried to give him a fairly decent funeral by digging up a fellow who was a sky pilot on the side. This preacher delivered a sermon on the prodigal son, which was about as good an alibi as could be made for a no-good cowboy. One old-timer said, "If that son of a bitch don't go to hell, there ain't no use having one."

But I had a more disagreeable problem on my hand that spring than a horse wrangler full of extract. The fact was I was getting a little too prosperous for some people. I had about 500 range horses with a yearly crop of 100 half-Percheron colts. Financially, I was in good shape, having a debt of only $2,000. A lot of the cattlemen had borrowed up to $10,000 on a book count of 500 critters, and as about half of them had disappeared, the ranchers owed more than their cattle would bring. I began to hear rumors that I had too many horses and that horses were as bad a nuisance on the range as sheep. A lot of this was just jealousy, because a horse would paw through the snow in the winter time and could range back in the hills a long way from water. While the cattle died or got scattered, my horse herd increased. In the twelve years I had been in South Dakota, I had gone from a wandering day laborer to a prosperous horse rancher. That is what hurt some of them.

My other trouble came over the Bar brand that was on some of my horses. The first broncs I bought had the Bar on the left shoulder. It could not be recorded as it was in conflict with many other brands. The old Wells Ranch had used it years before. Ben Ash bought the brand and had it on about 4,000 horses. Dave Crippen, who ran a feed barn in Fort Pierre, kept a small bunch of broncs on Willow Creek twenty-five miles northwest of Pierre, and these had the Bar on the left shoulder as the only brand. Judge Loring E. Goffey used the same mark on his several hundred horses between the Bad and Cheyenne rivers. Dozens of others used it as part of a recorded brand.

Neither Crippen nor Goffey kept a ranch or rode after their horses. Goffey's system was to pay a rancher one dollar a head for branding his colts and another dollar for delivering one to the Pierre stockyard. Crippen tried to get it done as an accommodation without pay. Well, his horses just disappeared. On my trips to town I had driven some of his strays to his pens, helped him brand and castrate colts, and made no charge for the work. When I kept my saddle horses in his corral, I always paid full price for it. One day when I went in, he accused me of stealing his Bar horses. As he was an old man, I didn't do any more than tell him what I thought of the deal, but I never spoke to him after this. Goffey asked me several times to bring in anything in the horse line with a Bar on the left shoulder, and he would pay me one dollar for my trouble. As I did not like the system of running horses all over the country and delivering them at that price, less the ferry fee at Pierre, I never delivered a single spavined old hammerhead. Some others like Goffey, who lived in town and ranched on the side, tried to keep track of their stuff by giving a rider a five-cent cigar and a glass of beer. Count me out on that kind of a deal.

One night about dark I came home and saw two horses tied up in the round corral. Herb Howland came out and said a couple of damned fools inside were looking for horses with a Bar on the left shoulder. They wanted grain for their horses and had even put their saddles in the house. We never fed anything but hay and never put a saddle in the shack. Herb had got supper for them and they were sprawled on his bed when I came in. One was a hulk of a boy about six-teen, and the other was an older man wearing the badge of a deputy sheriff. They were from the wheat-farming country over near Highmore and looked mighty funny wearing six-shooters and acting impudent-like. Herb rolled out a round-up bed for the guests that night, but they told him they did not like to sleep on the floor, so he let them have his bed and slept on the floor himself. I went outside to spend the night.

Herb was up early the next morning to get breakfast. He made extra-hard sinkers and weak coffee and served it with-out sugar or canned milk. There wasn't much talk during the meal until Herb told them they should file the sights off their guns. They both asked why, and Herb gave them the answer: "Why, someone might stick the barrels up your hind-end and kick the handles off." This was a worn-out gag to show the nonsense of would-be toughs carrying guns. Most sensible ranchers did not allow their cowhands to tote guns around.

When the toughs left, Herb followed them. In about an hour he came in on a run and said they had got the old gray stud and his bunch and were on the way to Pierre with them. I got out my Winchester and jumped on old Legs and started after them. Legs was a good running horse and fairly quiet to shoot off of. They were hurrying along on a trot when

I caught sight of them. The big one waved at me to go back but I pulled up to him and made a snap shot that hit his horse behind the ear, killing it dead. The boy began to cry and the one on the ground turned a dirty gray. I told the boy to get off, made both of them lay down their guns and told them to start moving. All their bluff was gone and they started out on a trot, one leading the horse, the other poking it along from behind. I heard they made it to Pierre without stopping or talking on the way. They may have even over-run Highmore before they slowed down to a stop. When I went home with the two guns, Herb wanted to know if I had killed them. I told him, "No, I just talked them out of their sinful ways."

This thing worried me, so I decided to go to Pierre and pick up the gossip. When I saw Louis La Plante on the street and told him the story, he laughed and told me to do nothing but keep my mouth shut, hang on to the pistols, and maybe see the banker who had a mortgage on the stock. Bert Cummins of the First National Bank listened to my story and told me the same. This made me feel a lot better, as I had never had any experience with courts or laws except when I once was a witness. Going home, I took a long running shot at a bobcat and killed it. The lower breeds of animal life—snakes, toughs, and bobcats—were getting scarcer around Pierre.

CHAPTER 13

BREAKING BRONCS AND GETTING EXPERIENCE

B REAKING BRONCS was a job that the boys who worked for me looked forward to every spring. We started in March and April while the horses were still weak and before the grass was green. The three- and four-year-olds wore down easy with all the throwing and tying, but the older ones were harder to handle. Even though I had a colt crop of about one hundred, we never had to break more than fifty a year. Cattlemen bought quite a few raw unbroke horses as well as green broke ones and paid me from thirty-five to fifty dollars for them. Some were broke to the wagon and

178

sold as work horses. All of this was great fun to my eighteen-year-old neighbor boys, and every one of them was worth two or three of the old-time wranglers. They were good at roping a bronc by the front feet and could ride most any of them without showing much daylight between the saddle and the seat of their pants.

The first thing we did at breaking time was to corral about ten of the broncs at a time and start in for a busy day. The colt was first thrown and his two front feet tied to a back one. A hackamore with a ten-foot rope was then put on and the horse allowed to get up. If he braced his feet when we pulled on the rope, we pulled him sideways to make him move or threw a loop over his rump so it would fall above the hock joint and give it a sharp jerk. This was like giving the horse a rap on the leg. One thing we never did do was to drag him straight ahead as that might hurt his neck so he could never hold his head up. A little petting and nose-rubbing helped him get the idea of leading.

The next step was to tie a loop around the bronc's neck at the shoulder, run the rest of the soft rope around a back leg and up to the loop where it was tied after pulling the leg off the ground. The horse was now on three legs and struggled to get loose. We would then fan him with a saddle blanket until he got used to it and made no fuss when it was dropped on his back. The saddle was put in its place and the single cinch drawn tight. He would do some bucking while the saddle was cinched, but he couldn't do much with one leg off of the ground. One of the boys would then take hold of the saddle horn from the left side but with the right hand and swing on, sit awhile, and get off. After doing this awhile, the bronc was worn down and could be led around carrying the saddle. One of us then made reins out of the hackamore rope and got on for the first ride around the corral. The bronc would buck a little and then settle down to practice

179

being guided right and left. After a few lessons like this, we took the horse outside the corral, snubbed him to a saddle horse which one of us rode, and started out. There was usually some bucking and then a good run. The next time the rider went it alone, and the bronc would do some fancy twisting to get rid of the saddle and rider. Mostly our riders had very little trouble staying on. The hardest horses to ride were the half-broke ones that had been out on green grass.

The horses were not the only weak ones in the spring. We always had a hunger for sour things. Before the breaking started, I would go to Pierre and get several gallons of pickles and a case of lemons. That carried us through the spring and satisfied everybody who came by.

By the summer of 1901, I had found all of my broncs that ran in the old Mississippi pasture of the reservation above the Cheyenne River, but thought I had a few out around it somewhere. After we had our haying done, I left Ray Chisholm in charge of our stock and started out to see what I could find. A fifty-dollar horse was worth looking for.

I started down the Cheyenne with two horses and came to Rousseau's place. He was one of the wealthy French-Indians and lived in a frame house on the reservation. When I rode up, a stylish-looking girl came out, dressed in a black silk dress and wearing nifty slippers—really a fine sight. She told me the men were gone, but I should put my horse in the lot and have dinner with her. You don't have to be coaxed to accept that kind of an invitation. After I had rested on the front porch awhile, she called, "Your dinner is ready." The table was well set with sterling silver, a big coffee and tea set, and a shiny platter. While I stowed away the food, she waited on table the way the half-breed women always did and talked a blue streak the way they didn't. Her name was Sophia, which sounded like a good handle for such a pretty girl. After staying about as long as I thought seemed proper, I started out to find the Rousseau roundup wagon, and when I left she invited me back for a fiddle dance sometime.

I found the Rousseau roundup bunch at the Goose Creek pens. It was a pretty good outfit. The cook, night wrangler, and two or three others were whites, the rest—about twenty-five—were Indians and mixed breeds. All in all it was a wild bunch, some of them even carrying six-shooters. These cowhands rode hard on circle, mostly on a lope in the first part and as fast as the cattle would run after that. They worked the herd every other day, sending cattle to the home range of the various reps who were there. After supper some of the wild young fullbloods would saddle their best cowhorses and practice roping and hog-tying the Texas steers. One would start out after a Longhorn on a hard run, drop the loop over his horns and flip the loose rope over the rump, then turn sharply to the left. This would bust the critter, and he would lie there unconscious with the wind knocked out of him. While the horse held the rope tight, the rider would get off and tie three legs. All of this was done in just a few seconds. Once in a while a steer's leg was broken or a horse was jerked off his feet, and the rider got up limping. Another pastime was to chase a steer, grab the tail and snub it around the saddle horn, then let loose. The animal would be thrown end over end and got up looking foolish.

Some of these riders were very cruel to their horses. They used both the "bear trap" bit that had a three- or four-inch spade running back into the horse's mouth or the "half-breed" that had a two-inch high part with a roller on it. Either of these could cause a horse to slobber and bleed at the mouth. The Mexicans and Spanish used the spade bit, too. With a few exceptions, the dark races were cruel to horses. White ranchers in South Dakota generally did not permit the use of such bits or any spurring or whipping in front of the saddle. I never used a spur at all in all the years I broke horses.

The cook told me a lot of windy stories while I was with this wild bunch, but he also tried to give me some good advice. He was afraid of some of the Indians who had Sitting Bull connections, and he slept with his revolver and a butcher knife under his pillow. Some of the breeds and fullbloods had sore eyes, which was mostly pox, he said, and he did not want me to use the big cotton sack towel used by the crew. He had been a sailor in China, Australia, and Africa, and a ranch hand in South America, so he was full of tales. Never get pox from a black man as it was sure and sudden death. Chinese women are cold-blooded so they have little stoves to warm them up some. The warmed-up ones cost twenty-five cents more. One crooked Chinese madam painted her stoves red to make them look hot. The cook thought she was a damned cheat. He is the one who told me the story about Harriet Lane, the Australian streetwalker. When the night guard changed every two hours, they would sit around the campfire, drink coffee and smoke cigarets, and talk about "towee," Sioux for sex. We could not understand much of what they said, but it seemed to be about the same as what all cowhands a long way from women talked about. There was a general belief in that country that eating so much beef whetted the sex desire and that when men went to the sporting houses they should take a drug so they could get satisfied for a long time without any female company. "Towee" was the most important topic of conversation in South Dakota.

After looking around there for four days, I decided none of my horses was in that part of the country, so with a lunch the cook packed for me, I set out southwest through the Sword and Dagger pasture. That outfit spent most of its time keeping the fence up and the strays out of that thirty- or forty-mile stretch. I spent the night with them but found none of my brands there. The next day I got to Benteen's store and post office, which was quite a civilized place. There was a woman cook and tables to eat off of. They had both ice water and ice cream. After getting a shave, haircut, and a shirt, I was ready to go back to Sansarc for a spell.

Not long after that, John Konzen came by and offered me $1,200 for twenty of my four- and five-year-old geldings. I took it and then started looking for a way to invest the money. One afternoon when I went to the Cheyenne to water my stock I saw a herd of two hundred horses, all thin, on the Cayuse order, and wearing Indian brands. The boy herding them was out of tobacco, so I gave him some and talked awhile. He said he was a Nez Percé from Lapwai, Idaho, and the horses belonged to three men who were then at Benteen's store. They had hired him at thirty dollars a month to help bring the herd from Jordan Valley, Oregon. On the way they had come through the Snake and Crow reservations, selling cheap whiskey, gambling, and trading horses with the Indians. When the outfit was near Ekalaka, Montana, the kid had got drunk and in a poker game had lost his horse and saddle as well as his wages. He was in real trouble—broke, homesick, scared of his bosses, and afoot one thousand miles from home in a country where it was disgraceful to walk.

I went up to Benteen's that night to see what they wanted for this herd. They offered them at fifteen dollars a head, colts thrown in, which was more than I would give. Ed Jones offered them eight dollars a head, but the owners said that was less than they cost them. He told them they had better go back to Oregon with them as Indian ponies were cheap in South Dakota and they would be hard to hold on a range here anyway. Sitting around in the Benteen bull pen or bunkhouse that night, these dudes talked of selling the herd in Fort Pierre and then going into the saloon and sporting house business. One of them who was a Texan wanted to go back home and fill a sporting house with colored wenches and really get rich. They talked a lot about their adventures with wild women and of fights they had had and made heroes of themselves. To me they looked like too mean a bunch to be allowed to live. They were sore at me when I told the boy to go to my place and I would give him a job for a while until he had enough money to go back home on a train.

I went on west to Frank Rood's place on Ash Creek, still looking for some horses to buy. He had a good house and a sixteen-year-old daughter, but the family was a little high-toned for the country. I bought seventeen wild broncs seventeen hands high and weighing from 1,500 to 1,700 pounds. If I had known how mean they were, I would not have paid $680 for them, as they were out of a bad stallion. Frank sent some kind of an educated Englishman to help me as far as Benteen's store, and we kept them on a lope most of the fifty miles. I offered the cowhand five dollars to help me on home with them, but he said he had had enough and turned back. It seemed to me the English were the worst foreigners we had in the United States.

The broncs were gaunt and thirsty after a day's run without water, so I drove them to the Cheyenne where they could fill out their sides. After drinking their fill, they waded out into the river and struck quicksand. They seemed bogged down for good. I went back to the store for help. Henry Hudson was there with a big team, but he refused to do any pulling as his horses were green broke. I was pretty sick of the job so went to the store and bought a box of cartridges for my revolver, which I had tied in my slicker on the back of the saddle. I blasted away from the bank but didn't hit any of them. When the shooting was over, the whole bunch was on the other side and I was out of the mess.

The Nez Percé boy started breaking them. He was a good

wrangler, like all the Indians of the mountain country, but these wildcats stumped him. They would bite, kick, and snort, and just wouldn't give in. Finally, I told Tommy, as we called the boy, we would drive the whole bunch to Pierre and try to sell them. On the way we stopped at Harry Hopkins' Road Ranch with these muddy-looking outlaws. Old Harry asked, "Where did you get all them big devils? Whoever gets them will be breaking them until Hell freezes over." I didn't argue the point. The next day in Pierre I sold the biggest one to Jim Turner, an ex-school teacher, for five dollars and took the rest of them across to Pierre on the ferry. They milled and snorted around and were big enough to see over the high fence around the boat. When old Cap Horn tooted the whistle, the horses had a fit. One old lady asked T. Madsen, another passenger, what made the horses so nervous, and he told her they got it from me and that all men and horses west of the Missouri were wild and might do anything.

We loaded this bunch into a thirty-six-foot car bedded down with sand and hay and I billed them to Canistota, South Dakota. While Tommy went back home, wearing the new clothes I bought him, I went with the train. The next afternoon, I unloaded in Canistota and went to a small hotel run by a young lawyer and his wife. This fellow put in a lot of time arguing with the loafers and would take either side of a question just to give him practice. He repeated some Latin phrases just to impress the listeners. One old man said the lawyer had studied Latin until he got to *non compos mentis* and quit. I had a good time with the girls while I was there, even if they had a ten o'clock curfew. When I got out with a young Canadian and the girls singing songs, I would have favored "Curfew Shall Not Ring Tonight."

The horse sales seemed slow so I billed a public sale. When the auctioneer had sold four at less than I paid for them, I stopped the sale. Then I hired a fellow to break four of them. He was so rough and cruel that three of them died, and the other one had his neck pulled down from dragging him. After that I decided to go back home across country with the rest of them. A constable followed me out of town and made me come back to bury the dead broncs. I back-tracked and paid a man fifteen dollars for putting the carcasses under the sod and then went and collected twenty dollars from the wrangler who killed them. I was anxious to get out of town.

That ride back would have been a heart-breaking one even if the temperatures hadn't been above 100 degrees. I made Alexandria the first night, where I stayed with a man I had met two years before when he was looking over the Sansarc country. After enjoying his artesian water and bathroom for a day, I went on, passed through Mitchell at noon and saw well-dressed folks sitting in the shade of the hotel with their noses up and looking at a sweaty horse wrangler. That night I had a good place to stay with a bachelor farmer and sold him one of the best horses for sixty-five dollars.

I spent the next night at Gann Valley in a good one-dollar-a-day hotel, then the next one in St. Stephen Catholic School. As it was vacation time, the Sister gave me the schoolroom to sleep in and cooked my meals for me. The young priest said he was lonesome and did a lot of visiting with me. The best luck I had was a day later when I traded the six wild broncs I had left to a rancher for a big black stallion. Now I would not have to face the Pierre people with a band of worthless horses, and they didn't need to know how much I had lost on the deal.

To make a long story short, I got to Fort Pierre finally, put the stallion in a feed barn for the winter, and went on home. The next spring I paid the stud's board bill of sixty dollars and turned him loose with a bunch of mares. He herded them a few days and then got killed in a fight with a gray stallion. I was out about five hundred dollars on the whole deal. After all, my place was at home branding colts and riding after strays. Experience comes a little high sometimes.

CHAPTER 14

THE BIG HORSE ROUNDUP OF 1902

IN THE FALL of 1901 there was a lot of talk about organiz-
ing a general horse roundup and getting all the scattered
broncs back to their home range. Horses had been so cheap
most of the years that many ranchers had not been willing
to do the riding that had to be done to keep them around
close. Branded mares with three- or four-year-old colts were
scattered all over the western part of Dakota. In my country
the only horse outfit that ran a wagon and roundup crew
was Narcelle. Several reps besides myself joined that wagon,
and I got back sixteen of the Rudy horses that Foster and I
had bought sight unseen.

188

To pass the time away I spent part of it in Pierre that winter. To make loafing easier, I dabbled in the wheat market at a bucket shop and after making $500, lost it and more too. I took a trip to Minneapolis and saw a good horse show for trotters, pacers, and ponies. Dan Patch, the fastest harness horse at that time, and some Hackneys, a nobby, stylish breed, also performed. Minneapolis had some good stage shows. I saw *Ben Hur*, which had real horses running on a tread mill, and others. After losing my money in the grain pit, I decided to go back to the sagebrush country where I belonged.

We set March 20, 1902, as the date for a meeting in Pierre to arrange for the big horse roundup. At that gathering, forty or fifty ranchers were there and everybody was enthusiastic about it. We elected Chas. Waldron president and Billy Moore secretary and treasurer.[1] There was some argument about what to do with the slicks. Someone said John Hayes claimed all of them for the Missouri River Stock Association and insisted on having them brought to Fort Pierre to him. Some argued that the ones found on their own range belonged to them. There was some heat about this, but the majority agreed to gather all the unbranded horses and to sell them to pay the expenses of the roundup. There were to be two outfits and each would need a cook, horse wrangler,

[1] The original members of the 1902 Horse Roundup Association, besides the officers, as taken from Sibert's notebook were D. Moore and Sons, A. C. Van Metre, Dan Powell, T. Madsen, C. W. McKinley, N. Welcome, N. Newbanks, A. A. Shoemaker, J. Beaver, Foster and Siberts, L. La Plante, Joe Valin, N. Narcelle, and A. H. Harvey. He says there may be others. In addition to the members, he had a long list of horse brands that people wanted gathered: Gus Seaman, 4 brands; Sam Curtis, 3; Ray Conklin, 6; Dick Mathieson, 5; Manuel Sylvia, 3; Wm. Dent, 5; A. Howes, Jr., 3; E. A. Morrison, 2; C. E. Lewis, 7; Chris Jenson, 2; Chas. Shannon, 8; E. J. Bartlett, 5; Henry Schact, 5; D. W. Bastion, 3; E. R. Gray, 1; A. C. Rickets, 1; N. J. Borden, 2; Louis Nichols, 1 old white horse with no brand; and many others. The above list is taken from six of the thirty-one pages of Sibert's notebook.

and night hawk, as well as a lot of grub and other things. This would cost some money and the sale of slicks would have to pay for it.

The plan was to work all the horses between the Cheyenne and White rivers, and west about 125 miles to the South Cheyenne. We elected Dan Powell as head foreman, and before I knew what was going on, Louis La Plante nominated me as the second in command to boss one crew. I was surprised and a little flattered to be elected, but actually it was only a headache that I got out of it. So many people wanted their brands gathered but were not willing to help in the roundup or to pay for delivering them to the stockyards at Pierre. A few did help us when we were in their country, and some were willing to pay all costs assessed against them. But these orders and demands to gather and take home all of the stray stock in western South Dakota to sixteen members of the Missouri Association made Dan Powell and me wonder who was running the roundup. The majority had agreed that we could not and would not run errands for everybody, and if they wanted their horses gathered, they could put up or shut up.

We set the starting time at May 17, a few days after the cattle roundups, so as not to get in their way and to give our saddle stuff a few more days on green grass. Dan was to take the inside wagon up and down Bad River, and I was to go south from Fort Pierre to Manuel Sylvia's corral on Antelope Creek, on to Medicine buttes, east to Chamberlain, and back to the north side of White River. I was to meet Powell's wagon at Lake Flat, about ten miles north of the present Wall. Then I was to go north to work the south side of the Cheyenne River, east to old Fort Bennett, and back to Fort Pierre where we would meet again and sort the two herds.

I went home after the meeting to get ready. As I was to furnish a team for the grub wagon, I got two big gray broncs in and hitched these wild ones together, which was the wrong thing to do. The right way to do it is to hitch a wild horse with a broke one. This team would run like deer every time we hitched them up. The boys liked the excitement and were a little sorry when we wore them down enough so they would run only a half-mile or so. One time they stampeded, ran into a water hole full of slush, and got so tangled up it took us two hours to unravel the mess. We gathered a dozen saddle broncs that looked like they would stand hard running and broke them. All of this kept us busy in April and early May. Before leaving for Fort Pierre on the twelfth, I hired Jim Jenson to stay at the ranch to herd two stallions and their bunches and to hold the strays that would be sent home from the roundup.

In Pierre I got Rex Terry to do my daytime horse wrangling, Charlie Howard for the night hawk, and Napoleon Welcome for cook. Welcome had an old grub box, a cupboard-like affair that fit into the back of the wagon to hold the dishes and small items. Roundup cooks had quit using Dutch ovens, so we got a sheet steel range, kettles to fit, and a complete set of cups, plates, and hardware, enough to feed twenty-five to fifty men. I let old Welcome do all of this as well as ordering the grub. I rigged up the wagon for a four-horse hitch, got the ropes and stakes for the saddle horse corral, and was ready to go on May 17.

We all helped hitch up the snorty horses, and old Welcome got hold of the lines. The team started on a dead run and the roundup begun. The pilot was ahead to guide the outfit, then came the wagon with the cook enjoying the ride, followed by the bed wagon, and a herd of about two hundred saddle horses. The first camp was made on Antelope Creek. Soon the riders were in with two hundred horses, most of them wearing the Wineglass brand of Sylvia, the Portuguese, who had a ranch near there. We cut his broncs out and penned them and had about sixty strays to hold in our herd. There were a lot of wobbly colts, and the mares worried over them all the time. A few stallions put on a bloody fight for us. Everybody was in good humor that day, and the boys did some fast and reckless riding.

The big gray lead team was wild and snorty the next day and ran for the first half mile on the way to Cedar Creek. This running seemed to start the day off right for the riders, but it worried me some as I did not want a spill. We camped at Smith's pens on the edge of the Lower Brule Indian Reservation. Several fullbloods came over that afternoon, wanting us to castrate some of their two- and three-year-old stallions as each was trying to corner a bunch of mares. It was quite a job, but we made it a rule to castrate all scrawny stock we got in the roundup unless somebody objected. In the two days there we gathered one hundred head and moved on to Medicine Creek, twenty miles west of Chamberlain.

After working a small bunch there and penning our herd of three hundred, the boys galloped off to Chamberlain to celebrate. It was always the custom to take some time off when a roundup got near town. By morning, all were back, having drunk a lot of whiskey, galloped through the streets, and acted as rowdy as the law allowed. Some showed the effects of town life. One fellow, called the Pigeon-Toed Kid, had a bad hangover and started to get mean with me. I called him down hard, and after that we got along pretty well.

When we crossed over to the reservation, we got an order from the agency to stay off, but we paid no attention to it. That was followed by another order to take all stray horses off the reservation and to castrate all the scrub stallions. As we were already doing this, it made no difference to us. We worked hard at the Medicine Butte camp but branded very few colts as they were too small. A big brand on a little colt is likely to blotch and be too big, so we cut the tail off square and let them go. We castrated and branded everything over a year old except breeding stallions.

Welcome, the cook, was opposed to cigaret smoking, and as the smokers used his matches, he had some reason to object. He said they could furnish their own matches and stay away from his kitchen with their coffin nails. The cook was the dictator around his cooking place, so no one could argue much with him. It was always a rule that a horse or a hairy saddle blanket could not be brought near the grub box. The big row about matches and cigarets kept on as long as Welcome cooked and got more bitter as the boys baited him. He claimed cigaret smoking was much worse than any perversion, and he decorated his language with good old four-letter words.

After another move or two, we had 500 or more horses gathered and had sent some to their home ranges. A lot of visitors dropped in, some to stay for a meal, others for several days. We had good grub but no beef to kill, and it was not the custom in these parts as it was in some places to kill colts to eat. When we moved to Bad River, we filled the corrals at the Hill Ranch and sent some in to Pierre to cut the size of the herd down to 250. Two days later at Midland, a town of 200 midway between Fort Pierre and Rapid City, the boys had another big celebration. There was drinking, dancing, and singing until things settled down after midnight. The oldest ones always got drunk, but the young ones kept their feet on the ground. About two o'clock there was a big uproar. Four of the older men were sleeping in a tent and one began to yell. He had fouled his bed and was blaming the others for it. It was finally agreed that the one who discovered it first was the cause of it. After that, the comedy was over and all was quiet.

Welcome had a good breakfast the next morning, but

mostly the hands wanted just coffee before riding off to the
next camp. The people of Midland were glad to see us go.
The easy money had been spent or lost in poker, and we had
worn out our welcome. We moved into the fine range country of Brave Bull Creek, where the U+ pens were. The
riders had lost some of their edge and were not as fast as
they had been the first few days, but we had six hundred in
the herd after we combed that range a couple of days. There
were a lot of 15-brand horses there but few slicks.

The 15 brand was owned by John Messingale, or Missouri John, and I had got a notice signed by the foreman,
John Rounds, not to round up any of their horses or use their
pens at Buffalo Creek. There were also some threats sent
in a roundabout way, but I paid no attention to them as I had
often been threatened with getting shot or licked or run out
of the country. At Midland we had a lot of this brand in the
U+ pens and looked for someone to come and object, but
nobody ever showed up. We went on to Missouri John's
pens on Buffalo Creek, even if some of the boys were afraid
of his Wyoming riders, who had a reputation of being tough.
This was a good set of pens. There was a big one that would
hold about 3,000 horses and two smaller work corrals. For
four days we worked in this part of the Bad Lands, and no
one ever bothered us.

Just as we were leaving, a young fellow rode up and said
Missouri John wanted to see me. I asked what for. He said
both Missouri John and his partner, Ross, were friendly and
just wanted to talk to me. I had known of these men since
1897. That was the year of the big horse race in Fort Pierre
which John and Ross won by a crooked deal. After the race
John's rider sold them out, and Ross told me, "We will go
home and round up a trainload of cattle. We have lost all
our money." Ross was the quiet type, but Big John was the
windy, old-style Westerner on the noisy order. Now as boss

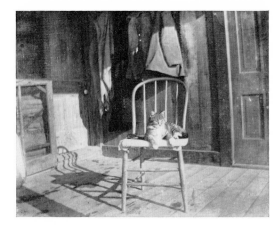

"Tom"

Bruce and Rose Siberts at the XO Ranch house

of a horse roundup on their range I was ordered to go see the big operators of the Bad Lands.

Leaving David Moore to boss the crew while they moved, I rode to the mouth of Fifteen Creek on White River. They had a well-fixed ranch with a big log house, bunkhouse, corrals, sheds, and stable. Two young fellows were in the blacksmith shop working with a lot of hay tools when I rode in. They put my horse in a pen, threw in some hay, and offered to feed him grain, but I told them the bronc had never had any in his life and we had better not start now. Missouri John was in the house, they said, and for me to go on in.

I went to the door and hollered, "Hello." John came to the door, shook hands, and invited me in. As we sat there, he did most of the talking. He remembered the race in 1897 when he and Ross had won the race but lost $6,000 when their rider double-crossed them, and John thought it a good joke on them now. He said he had a good sorrel Thoroughbred stallion out of Lexington stock and took me out to see him. When we went back to the house, he got out a jug of whiskey, and we talked more about horses. About noon he went to the door and called to the young fellows to come on up and let's have something to eat. After filling up on ham, peaches, and a lot of good food, he got out the cigars and we talked some more. When I told him I had to go, he gave me a handful of cigars, and as I started out, he hollered, "Wait!" I looked in, and he pulled a trunk out from under the bed, got a box of cigars out, and told me to take them to the boys. He followed me to the corral and talked as I got on my horse. After I had got away a few rods, I looked back and waved at him. He took off his old hat and waved it at me as he laughed. I decided that old John wasn't quite the devil he was made to be. Rounds, the foreman, was really the bluffer all the time.

When we had agreed on this roundup, Chas. Waldron was to furnish a lead team for the grub wagon, and McKinley was to furnish four horses for the bed wagon. A dozen others volunteered to lend us two or three horses apiece for the wrangler and night hawk. But some of them didn't come through. I had to hire a lead team for the bed wagon, and Welcome brought his team to hitch with mine on the grub wagon. No one sent a saddle horse for the day and night herders. I had to give them some of mine and that left me short. We had picked up some strays of people I knew, so I used them and never charged any of them for bringing their broncs home. Near Chamberlain we had found a horse belonging to the Mississippi Ranch one hundred miles away, and we put him on the bed wagon. I heard that Jeff Carr of the Mississippi Ranch was mad about this and said he was going to give me a damn good licking. I sent word that I would be looking for the son of a bitch, but he never showed up.

At several camps we had cases of lockjaw tetanus. Horses' jaws would get solid after a long run. Welcome said he knew how to cure it. He had us throw the animal, put a board on its forehead, then hit the board a hard lick with the blunt end of an ax or sledge. This treatment cured all the cases we had, and it made Dr. Welcome so pleased that he got a bit uppity.

Home remedies had to cure everything when I was in South Dakota. There was a vet in Pierre nicknamed Dr. Horse, who had a diploma but wasn't of much use as he was drunk all the time. In the winter he slept in the manure back of the livery barn. He said the heat kept him quite warm. We just got along without horse doctors and cured them by guess and by God. If maggots got in a wire cut, we left them alone and they ate the dead flesh. We even knew how to make spots on a horse. Cook a potato twenty minutes, cut it in half, and apply the flat part where you want the spot. If done right, there will be a white spot scald there. If I told how broncs were changed in other ways, someone might try it and get in the pen.

The roundup moved on from Whitewater Creek and Sage Creek to Lake Flat, where we met Dan Powell's wagon with about 2,000 horses. We put some of our 300 or 400 in his herd and took some of his that belonged in the direction we were going. As the grub wagons were low on supplies, he and I took a four-horse team and went to Smithville at the mouth of Elk Creek where Frank Cattle had a store and a road ranch. Most hands ordered whiskey, but we didn't bring back enough for a general drunk. We had too many horses to hold for that kind of a celebration.

After working Deep Creek and Squaw Creek, we moved to Frank Rood's place on Ash Creek, where we had good pens. Frank was away on a cow roundup, but Mrs. Eva Rood and Hazel were there. Mrs. Rood invited me to dinner, or as she said, "dinnah." She was from New Jersey and was quite an entertainer and a dancer. Once a fellow was telling a neighbor how high Eva could kick when she danced. An oldish woman there said she was some kicker, too. The old gal histed her skirt and kicked the ridge pole but fell backward and broke her arm. Eva didn't do any kicking for me, but she set a nice table with cut glass, china, extra-good food, and a lot of style. Several years later when Frank was elected secretary of state, Eva had a chance to play society. I called on her once in Pierre and she told me a lot of her experiences with the state house crowd. She was a rose out in the South Dakota sagebrush.

Billy Moore said he had been lost all the time we were in the Bad Lands and on Deep Creek, but from there on he said he knew the country like a book. I had him pilot the wagon to Plum Creek. He got lost, and got to where he should have been at noon in time for a late supper. The men were hungry and peevish and kidded him so much that he quit as pilot. It was easy to get lost out where there was so much prairie and sky, and there was hardly anybody who didn't get lost at some time or other.

We worked a lot of small bunches on Plum Creek and did a lot of castrating of scrub Indian stock. Horses were sent home in all directions, as this was the last big roundup before going to Fort Pierre. I got a chance to shave and clean up in the three days there. We moved to McLain and Williams' corral near Standing Butte and worked the country around Fort Bennett and to the mouth of the Cheyenne, then with the wagon horses at a trot we pulled into Fort Pierre on June 25.

The stockyards were jammed with the 3,000 or more horses. After a big sale the next day we still had 2,000 left. They were belly deep in mud and had no feed or water. The owners were in the saloons, and some were pretty drunk. The railroad hired a man to haul the dead broncs out of the yards and dump them in the Missouri. I think I got the blame for everything—the rain, the dead horses, and bringing slicks from every range we found them on. I did not stay to listen to a lot of bellyaching as I was through as boss of the 1902 roundup and decided that once was enough in one lifetime. Maybe if I came back to earth as a jack rabbit sometime, I might try it again. So with twelve slicks and six branded horses, I struck out across the prairie. I always did like broncs better than I did a lot of men.

CHAPTER 15

BLIZZARDS AND HOMESTEADERS

I N THAT big country west of the Missouri we never saw
anything but the cabins of ranchers before 1902. Then
the claim shacks began to show up on the level land near the
trails and roads. The wool-hat people with their kids and
plows had come. Some of the ranchers tried to hold on to
the water holes and the hay bottoms by hiring somebody to
file on them. The going price was $200 for building an eight-
by-ten shack and putting a stove and a cot in it. Then there
were others who made a claim in order to sell out to anybody
who came along. Some boasted they had never slept on their

claim at all, and the Land Office never pried much into such personal affairs. After Teddy Roosevelt became president, I heard there were quite a lot of prosecutions for fraud, but I never saw many convicted around me for making a final proof out of just plain blue sky. But the sod-busters, including a lot of schoolteachers out to pick up some change, were there to stay, and the wide-open prairie that we had used for free pasture was on the way out forever.

By 1906, when I left South Dakota, the homesteaders were pretty thick. Sometimes they built a cluster of shacks on the corners of four quarter-sections just so they could have company. Right south of me a cigar-maker made a claim, and across at Rider's Butte his mother-in-law built herself a shack. He sold cigars around the country and did pretty well. Another settler, Riley Dunkleberger, had a claim not far from Rider's Butte. Six miles south of my ranch was Johnson, who was actually a farmer. He had cows, chickens, a team, and seven kids. To keep alive, he worked around the country wherever he could, and as he was an ex-barber, he cut hair for all the men on Sansarc. After Mrs. Johnson started doing my laundry, I probably looked better than I ever had since I went to South Dakota. Sometimes when Johnson would get low on grub, he would come to me to get a loan. I would give him thirty or forty dollars, and off he went to the store to get his beans and bacon. Sometimes he got mixed up and would get mostly a caddy of tobacco and a quart of whiskey. He said he would be perfectly happy if he could just have a drink now and then. When I needed someone to work for me, he would come and work off his debt at $1.50 a day and his meals.

Just south of the Johnsons were the Woodards—Ed, Estella, and Rose—and the Jake Argenbrights. They had four claims together and lived in shacks only a few rods apart. On the south Sansarc the Johnston Jeffries and their ten kids had a place. He was a claims locator for the home-steaders who came in, getting twenty-five dollars for spot-ting a good place and about thirty dollars for building a shack on the land. West of my ranch was the claim of S. O. Norvald. He had come to South Dakota in the 1880's from Norway and published a Norwegian-language weekly newspaper for a while. There were several young lady claim-holders around there, some from the East who might have been looking for husbands as much as for land. Young Jim Jeffries and I used to ride around to find the best-lookers who might need help. One day we found two and had a long visit. Jim saw some sacks full of something and asked what was in them. They didn't answer, so he went and opened one sack. I asked what was in it, and he said it looked like fuel. It was cow chips. The girls blushed and said they used gloves to handle the fuel. I think this was overdoing it as the cow-piles were sun cured, and I never heard of any bad effects from using them. It was the main fuel in lots of places and the only fuel in some.

West of me between the Sansarc and Willow Creek was a bare prairie quite a way from water or wood. Some-how, a family from Chicago decided to strike it rich by filing there. As the Kellars had a grown daughter as well as two small boys, I naturally had an extra-special interest in them, but the ranchers generally talked pretty bad about all of them. Most of it was talk, as they knew that the home-steader had an honest right to lay claim to vacant land. But any time a rancher could do anything to bother them he did. One day Big Nose Marion came by the Kellars' and saw their water barrel out in the open, the one they used to haul water from the creek, so he threw it on the wagon and started off. When Kellar saw it was gone, he started out afoot after Big Nose and caught him down the trail a few miles. I don't know just what happened, but he did get the barrel and rolled it five miles back to his shack. The Kellars stuck it out and made good in one way or another, but Big Nose soon got out of the cattle business and ended up as a janitor in a school somewhere in the Black Hills.

The free range was getting pinched, not only by the homesteaders but also because there were too many mouths to feed on the prairie that was left. The cattlemen hadn't made any money for years, so they quit one by one. Some went back east, some went into business in town, and others moved their herds up to Canada and started out again there. Very few had a fortune when they folded up. The sheepmen had always done better than the cattlemen, but they felt the same squeeze west of the Missouri after about 1904 or 1905.

I had been doing all right with horses. The colt crop was good every year, and the prices had done pretty well after the Boer War sent them up. In June, 1902, I shipped a carload to DeWitt, Iowa, and averaged between fifty and seventy-five dollars apiece. They were sold at an auction back of a saloon, and I'll admit that the drinks helped some. That August I tried it again but didn't do so well. There had been a ball game at DeWitt the day before, and it had ended up in a fight. This hurt my sale, so I decided to try some other place after that.

In the fall of 1904 I shipped two carloads to East St. Louis, the biggest horse market in the world at that time. They had pens for thousands of horses and sold several carloads a week to buyers from all over the world as well as from the East. While I was there, I went to see the World's Fair in St. Louis. It was not quite as big as the one in Chicago in 1893, but there was still lots to see and a lot of walking to do. I had my first ride in an automobile bus that toured the fairgrounds, and even though it cost two dollars, I thought it had something on a horse for sight-seeing. Back in Pierre with $2,000 for the forty-five broncs, I could now look even the banker in the eye.

It was the winter and spring of 1904–1905, as well as the homesteaders, that finally got my goat in South Dakota. That fall and winter were very dry. I turned the horses north of the Cheyenne and chopped holes in the ice all winter so they could have water. Anyone living in a draw built a dam to catch any run-off, but none ever came. We didn't have much sickness those days as the winter killed all the germs and the hot summers finished them off, but the weather sure was a problem. The May blizzard nearly done all of us in.

It had been dry and warm in April of 1905. The little colts were in good shape, and most of the grown horses had lost their winter coat of shaggy hair. The wolves had killed a few colts, and I had hired Levi Moore to come and trap what he could, giving him ten dollars for every one brought in. With the state bounty of ten dollars he was doing pretty well, and I liked to have him around. On May 1, a cold rain came. On the second, it was colder and some wet snow fell. The next day the temperature dropped below freezing. On the fourth and fifth, zero weather and a blizzard moved in on us from the Rockies. Levi and I never left the cabin except to get wood and water. We picked up some larks near the shack and brought them in, but they died. About all we could talk about was what damage the storm would do. Levi believed it would kill some cattle but not horses, but that every sheep in the country would be dead and in that way it would be a good thing.

It was clear and sunny on May 6, and the snow was melting. We went to the horse pasture to see about Levi's nice team of buckskin horses and found them in the corner —dead. The saddle horses that had some of their winter coat on yet were still alive. We walked to a butte through foot-deep snow and over drifts five to ten feet high and could see dead stock in every direction. Some of the neighbors were already out skinning. In the next few days we found thirty-five of my broncs dead along a wire fence south of the place. Some of them were baby colts which had been slick and pretty only a few days before. I lost all in all about 300 horses out of a herd of around 800 and felt pretty sick about it. Jim Cox had turned loose 2,000 steers on Lake Flat north of the Bad Lands. They drifted to the wall and went over in piles. He found about 99 per cent of them dead. Cattle and horse losses were mostly from 50 to 90 per cent. As if this wasn't bad enough, a flood came in early July, took out my dam on the Sansarc which had cost me about four hundred dollars in labor, and drowned a few more horses.

This was the last straw. A blizzard is bad enough in winter, but when it comes in May and is followed up with a flood, I figured Old Johnny God wasn't doing right by me. I decided to get the hell out of South Dakota.

We started rounding up the stock and shipping it out. McCreary and Carey of the Union Stockyards of South Omaha offered me twenty-eight dollars a head, colts thrown in, for all I would deliver between September 1 and 15. We made a big drive and got about five hundred, leaving only six broke horses, one stallion, about forty wire-cut and other cripples, and a few scattered ones we couldn't find. After this deal was over, I had my ranch and my cripples left and $20,000 in the bank with all debts paid. I was a free man.

Leaving Jim Jenson in charge of the place, I went south to find a new location where blizzards didn't come in May. At Fayetteville, Arkansas, I stopped to look over the country. A real estate agent took me around. The farms weren't so good, but the orchards were fine. The people were friendly after the shyness wore off. Some of the farmers were talking a lot about raising long-eared jackasses, and those that had fifty or a hundred head were doing pretty well. It was a pleasant country to live in but not to make money to any amount. When I told the real estate agent that I guessed I wouldn't buy, he was peeved, said he wanted only good people to come and help improve the country.

I went on to Springfield, Missouri, where my Uncle Norm Terry lived. He was a good-looking doctor with a big practice. After being shot up in Lyons, Kansas, by a jealous husband, he had moved to Springfield and helped promote the first hospital operations on goiter. My folks always said his trouble in Kansas was without cause, but I doubt it. Aunt Leora was prim and prissy, a typical aristocrat of the South, and rode around in a glass-enclosed carriage with an outside seat for the driver. A colored man slept in the barn to take care of the horses, and a white maid looked after the house. While I was there, Uncle Norm acted as driver and I was the footman for Aunt Dora in one of her trips about town. When we got back, she told us we didn't match up to the job very well.

When Uncle Norm died at fifty-eight, I went to his funeral. An old southern preacher gave a talk about a black man having no soul and proved it from the Bible where it spoke of beasts of the field. Uncle Norm's brother, Stew, who was deaf as a post, disagreed when we told him what the preacher said. The other brother, Jim, more than disagreed. He swore and said, "By God, I am a John Brown Republican." The whole funeral was quite a success. All in all, my relatives were a pretty good show.

After looking around in Missouri, I went to Boulder, Colorado, where my brother Aubrey had moved to fight T. B. He wasn't doing so well as most of the doctors were a bunch of quacks just taking money. I went to a football game between the universities of Colorado and Kansas. A colored man played on the Kansas team and everybody was a good sport about it. That was lots different than the bellyaching I heard at the Arkansas game. Scrubs are scrubs wherever you find them, and Arkansas had more than its share.

Back at my XO Ranch on the Sansarc it seemed lonesome without the horses, even if I had some pretty girls as neighbors. I had a buggy and hauled the homesteaders around some. Rose Woodard and I seemed to hit it off the best. One night after staying at her claim until quite late, I went to sleep driving home. When I woke up the team was running in circles at a fast clip. I was afraid of a spill, but they finally ran down and stopped.

Another time when Rose and I were riding around the prairie, we went to where some old maids had their shacks together. No one was around so we went quiet-like up to the window. They all had their fingers up in front of their faces counting one, two, three, four, five. That was as far as they got when we tapped on the window. They all jumped and screamed, upset the lamp, and when we went in, gave us quite a scolding. The counting of the fingers was their calculation about a couple producing a baby in five months. After the first outburst they all agreed not to be mad if we would not mention that we had seen them counting fingers. These old maids with their screwed up mouths was about the best picture I ever had of virgins gossiping. After all, a five-month baby is not a world's record by any means.

On the night of December 13, 1905, Rose and I were married in the Methodist parsonage at Pierre. The next morning when we got on the train to go to Omaha, Scotty Phillips, who had the buffaloes, was on. He called Rose "Mrs. Siberts," which seemed to shock her. We doubled back to Colorado to look around for a ranch to buy, but finding it cold and snowy there, we decided to go on south. I had heard that oil had been discovered in Oklahoma so went to Okmulgee and bought a place twenty-five miles south of the first big oil pool. I figured one might raise some oil as well as horses in a place like that. Besides, it had the best water I had tasted in the south, and I was tired of alkali after living fifteen years in South Dakota.

When spring came and the ice went out of the Cheyenne with a boom that could be heard fifteen miles, I put Rose on the train and began to round up the leavings out of my big herd of horses. Jim Jenson and I found a carload, and we billed them for Oklahoma. I went along in the caboose. In the Kansas City yards I sold a showy pinto horse to an old medicine man with long hair and a goatee for $100, the highest price I had ever got up to that time. At Sapulpa, Indian Territory, we stopped overnight to feed and water the stock. I slept in the train dispatcher's office. In the night I heard a lot of shooting and heard that a colored woman had shot and killed four white men in a resort near the depot. It must have been some job to mop up after all that.

After getting settled down that summer, I went back to South Dakota to sell my ranch and anything else I could find around. Florence Jeffries bought the 160 acres for $800, with $300 down. Riley Dunkleburger bought a Percheron stallion for $200, and Charlie Howard took the forty-five horses left at twelve dollars apiece with the colts thrown in. The ranch business went a little sour later, and Florence forfeited the down payment she had made. I sold the ranch again to her son, Jim, who had worked for me, for $500, and that finished my ranching days in South Dakota.

It is all over now. As I look over the 8,000 acres in Oklahoma land I have now and think about the days when I lived in my little cabin on the Sansarc, I can see that it was horses that gave me my start. If I had stayed in cattle, I might still have been drinking alkali water and living with a mortgage in South Dakota. But it wasn't a bad place for a young man to start out—even if there was nothing but prairie and sky.

INDEX

Abear, Raymond: on roundup, 62–63; story about, 109
Agnew, Sandy, rewards Siberts: 69
Angel, Henry: has store, 19; loses heifer, 75
Anthony, Susan B., appearance of: 118
Argenbright, Jake, homesteader: 200
Army, U. S., at Plum Creek: 25–28
Ash, Ben C., horse rancher: 16, 81, 132, 175

Bacon, Chauncy: 118
Badger, eaten at Williams: 62
Barnes, Snyder, death of: 92

Jeffries, Johnston, homesteader: 200–201
Jenson, Chris, roundup association member: 189n.
Jenson, Jim, works for Siberts: 141, 191, 204
Johnson County, Wyoming, range war of: 31, 54
Johnson family, homesteaders: 200
Jones, Ed. buys horses: 156, 183
July 4, celebration of: 102–104

Keller family, homesteaders: 201–202
Kennedy, Dr., rancher: 60–61
Konzen, John, bought Siberts' horses: 183
Kruder, Mary E., servant girl: 91

Lampe, Frank, disappearance of: 68
Lane, Harriet, story of: 2
La Plante, Louis, in horse roundup: 189n., 190
Larson, Ole, Siberts drinks with: 128–29
Legislature, South Dakota, in session: 37–38, 164
Leslie Post Office: site of, 19; dance at, 155–56
Lewis, C. E., roundup association member: 189n.
Lice, getting rid of: 11
Lighton, Jim, Missouri ferry of: 66
Lindsay Post Office: 168, 173
Little Bear: cabins of, 27; wives of, 32; Siberts' neighbor, 69,
    71–72
Lucky Bill, episode of: 173–74
Lyman, Ed, Narcelle's wagon boss: 151–54

McCleary and Carey, commission firm: 204
McGaff, John, rancher: 148, 163
McKinley, C. W., roundup association member: 189n.
McLain and Williams, corral of: 198
Madsen, T.: 185; roundup association member, 189n.
Madsen ranch, Siberts works for: 93
Marion, Big Nose, steals barrel: 201–202
Marrington, Elton, disappearance of: 68
Marrington ranch: 47; roundup of, 65

UNIVERSITY OF OKLAHOMA PRESS
NORMAN